Quest

Listening and Speaking in the Academic World, Book 1

Pamela Hartmann
Los Angeles Unified School District

Laurie Blass

Boston   Burr Ridge, IL   Dubuque, IA   Madison, WI
New York   San Francisco   St. Louis
Bangkok   Bogotá   Caracas   Lisbon   London
Madrid   Mexico City   Milan   New Delhi   Seoul
Singapore   Sydney   Taipei   Toronto

McGraw-Hill Higher Education

A Division of The **McGraw-Hill** *Companies*

QUEST: LISTENING AND SPEAKING IN THE ACADEMIC WORLD, BOOK 1

This book is printed on acid-free paper.

1 2 3 4 5 6 7 8 9 0 QPF/QPF 0 9 8 7 6 5 4 3 2 1 0

ISBN 0–07–006249–8

Vice president and editorial director: *Thalia Dorwick*
Publisher: *Tim Stookesberry*
Developmental editor: *Aurora Martinez Ramos*
Marketing manager: *Pam Tiberia*
Project manager: *Joyce M. Berendes*
Production supervisor: *Sandy Ludovissy*
Designer: *Michael Warrell*
Senior photo research coordinator: *Carrie K. Burger*
Supplement coordinator: *Sandra M. Schnee*
Compositor: *David Corona Design*
Typeface: *10/12 Times Roman*
Printer: *Quebecor Printing Book Group/Fairfield, PA*

Cover designer: *Victory Productions*
Cover image: *Lonnie Sue Johnson*
Photo research: *Toni Michaels*
Illustrator: *ElectraGraphics, Inc.*

The credits section for this book begins on page 224 and is considered an extension of the copyright page.

INTERNATIONAL EDITION ISBN 0–07–116387–5

www.mhhe.com

contents

preface

Quest: The Series

The *Quest* series addresses the need to prepare students for the demands of college-level academic coursework. *Quest* differs from other content-based ESOL series in that it incorporates material typically covered in general education courses, and contains a variety of academic areas including biology, business, U.S. history, psychology, art history, anthropology, literature, and economics.

    Quest has been designed to parallel and accelerate the process that native speakers of English go through when they study core required subjects in high school. By previewing typical college course material, *Quest* helps students get "up to speed" in terms of both academic content and language skills.

    In addition, *Quest* prepares students for the daunting amount and level of reading, writing, listening, and speaking required for college success. The three *Reading and Writing* books combine high-interest material from newspapers and magazines with traditional academic source materials such as textbooks. Reading passages increase in length and difficulty across the three levels. The *Listening and Speaking* books in the *Quest* series contain listening strategies and practice activities based on recorded conversations among college students, authentic "person-on-the-street" interviews, radio programs, and college lectures. Similar to the *Reading and Writing* books, the three *Listening and Speaking* books increase in difficulty within each level and between levels.

    The *Quest Listening and Speaking* books have been coordinated with the *Reading and Writing* books so that the two, used in conjunction, provide students with complementary, overlapping, yet distinct information—much as happens in a typical college class, in which students attend a lecture on a given topic and then complete textbook reading assignments on a related topic.

Quest: Listening and Speaking in the Academic World, Book 1

Quest: Listening and Speaking the Academic World, Book 1 begins with an introductory chapter, Getting Started. This chapter presents basic information about higher education in the United States and Canada and introduces students to the concept of listening and speaking in a college context; included is practice in taking lecture notes, listening for the main idea, and understanding fast or difficult English—areas covered in all subsequent chapters at increasingly challenging levels.

    Following the introductory chapter are three distinct units, each focusing on a different area of college study—business, biology, and U.S. history. Each content unit contains two chapters. The business unit is comprised of chapters on career planning (beginning college) and the free enterprise system, and the biology unit includes chapters on animal behavior and nutrition. The chapters in the last unit, on U.S. history, concentrate on slavery in the United States and on Native Americans in the 19th century.

Unique to this series is the inclusion of three different *types* of listening passages in each chapter:

- Everyday English—an informal conversation among college students (or in some chapters, person-on-the street interviews)—on both audiotape and videotape;
- Broadcast English—an authentic radio segment from such sources as National Public Radio and Public Radio International; and
- Academic English—a short college lecture.

Unique Chapter Structure

Each chapter of *Quest: Listening and Speaking in the Academic World, Book 1* (with the exception of Getting Started) contains five parts that blend listening, speaking, and academic skills within the content of a particular area of study. In Part One, pictures, charts, and/or a short reading provide the basis for discussion and journal writing and prepare students for the listening passages that follow. In Part Two, Everyday English, students listen to and use informal, conversational English related to the chapter theme. Part Three, The Mechanics of Listening and Speaking, focuses on language function, pronunciation, and intonation; it culminates in an activity requiring students to make use of all three of these areas. In Part Four, Broadcast English, students learn—at even the level of Book 1—to understand and discuss an authentic radio passage which, in turn, helps to prepare them for the lecture that follows. Part Five, Academic English, presents an audiotaped lecture on the chapter theme and guides students toward proficient note-taking skills; the final activity in the chapter, Step Beyond, involves students in discussion, original research, and presentation of their own findings.

Supplements*

The Instructor's Manual to accompany *Quest: Listening and Speaking in the Academic World, Books 1-3* provides instructors with a general outline of the series, as well as detailed teaching suggestions and important information regarding levels and placement, classroom management, and chapter organization. For each of the three books, there is also a separate section with answer keys, oral practice, and unit tests. In addition, there is an audio/video component to accompany each of the three *Quest: Listening and Speaking* books. Tapescripts are also available.

Acknowledgments

Many, many thanks go to those who have made and are making this series possible: Marguerite Ann Snow, who provided the initial inspiration for this entire series; publisher for ESOL, Tim Stookesberry, who first said *yes;* vice president and editorial director Thalia Dorwick, who made it happen; editors Janet Battiste and Aurora Martinez Ramos, who gave encouragement and support and helped shape the manuscript; marketing manager Pam Tiberia, who guides the books into classrooms; Joe Higgins of National Public Radio, who went above-and-beyond to help us find one especially wonderful but elusive tape; the many students who have tried materials and let us know what worked and what didn't; the good people at Mannic Productions; the entire production team in Dubuque; and the following reviewers, whose opinions and suggestions were invaluable: Marietta Urban, Karen Davy, and Mark Litwicki.

* The supplements listed here accompany *Quest: Listening and Speaking in the Academic World, Books 1-3.* Please contact your local McGraw-Hill representative for details concerning policies, prices, and availability as some restrictions may apply.

visual tour
Highlights of this Book

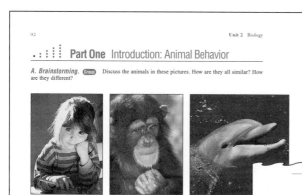

Part One: Focus on Activating Prior Knowledge with Practice Opportunities in all Language Skills

Part One of each chapter contains a variety of high-interest activities that gradually introduce students to the chapter topic. In these examples, students are given the opportunity to discuss what they already know about animal behavior and to read a brief passage about anecdotes that depict animal behavior. This section is typically followed by discussion questions and ends with a journal writing activity in which students share their reactions to the chapter topic or their knowledge of the subject matter. (pages 92 and 93)

Page 92:

92   Unit 2 Biology

Part One Introduction: Animal Behavior

A. Brainstorming. (Group) Discuss the animals in these pictures. How are they all similar? How are they different?

A human   A chimpanzee   A dolphin

Page 93:

Strange but True

Sheba is a healthy six-year-old. She is learning many things: to choose colors, to count (from zero to seven so far), to know words for body parts, and to take care of her own pet dog. Sheba is a chimpanzee.

　　　　　* * * * * *

In Kenya, vervet monkeys make many different noises. Some of these noises are alarm calls—"Danger!" One call means "Snake!" When the monkeys hear this, they all look down. A different call means "Leopard!"
5 The monkeys hear this, and they run into the trees. A third call means "Eagle!" At this call, all the monkeys look up into the sky.

　　　　　* * * * * *

On July 23, 1996, Martin Richardson was on a tourist boat off the coast of Egypt. A group of dolphins was jumping playfully near the boat. Richardson and two friends decided to swim with the dolphins, and they jumped into the water. Suddenly, a shark appeared and attacked Richardson. Soon the water was red
10 with his blood. Immediately, three of the dolphins swam around him. They began to hit the water again and again with their tails. They protected Richardson from the shark and saved his life.

Sources: Story of Sheba the chimpanzee, adapted from Sally Boysen, "Proving a professor's pet theory, Sheba the Chimp is treating a basset hound as her own dog" from *People Weekly* (April 18, 1988). Copyright © 1988 by Time, Inc. Reprinted with the permission of *Time*.

Story of vervet monkeys, adapted from Marian Stamp Dawkins, "The private life of the vampire bat . . . and other surprising examples of animal behavior" from *UNESCO Courier* (February 1988). Copyright © 1988 by UNESCO (France). Reprinted with the permission of the publishers.

Story of Martin Richardson and dolphins, adapted from Aline A. Newman, "Animals in action" from *Boys' Life* (March 1998) 88, no. 3. Copyright © 1998 by the Boy Scouts of America, Inc. Reprinted with the permission of *Boys' Life*.

C. Discussion. (Group) Discuss your answers to these questions.

1. Did anything in "Strange but True" surprise you? If so, what?

2. What do the three examples in the reading show us about animals' ability to communicate, their intelligence, and their emotions?

3. Do you know any other strange-but-true animal stories? If so, tell one to your group.

D. Journal Writing. Choose *one* of these topics. Write about it for five minutes. Don't worry about grammar and don't use a dictionary. Just put as many ideas as you can on paper.

• Write your ideas about one of the animals from "Strange but True."

• Describe an animal that a classmate told you about.

• Tell a story about any other surprising animal.

94   Unit 2   Biology

.:::: **Part Two** Everyday English: That Darn Cat

Before Listening

A. Brainstorming. Group   Talk about these animals. What do you know about their ability to communicate, their intelligence, and their emotions?

A domestic cat   A domestic dog   Humans

Emphasis on Listening Preparation
All listening passages are preceded by prelistening activities such as brainstorming, discussion, prediction, and vocabulary preparation. In this example, students engage in a brainstorming session that will prepare them for the listening passage found later in this part of the chapter. (page 94)

Chapter Three   Animal Behavior   95

C. Discussing Survey Results. Group   Discuss the results of the survey. Try to answer these questions:

1. Do most people with pets think that animals feel emotions?
2. Do most people without pets think that animals feel emotions?
3. Are the two groups' ideas similar?
4. Do most people think that animals feel emotions?

Listening

A. Listening for the Main Idea. Video/Audio   Listen to the conversation. As you listen, try to answer this question:

• What do Tanya, Jennifer, and Brandon believe about animals' emotions and intelligence?

B. Listening for Reasons. Video/Audio   Read these questions. Then listen to the conversation again. Write your answers.

Icons Provide Clear Instruction
All speaking activities in the book are labeled for pair, group, or class practice. Listening activities are accompanied by icons that tell whether the materials are available in audio or video formats—or both. (page 95)

C. Listening for Stressed Words. Video/Audio   Listen again to part of the conversation. Fill in the blanks with the stressed words. Use the words in the box.

animals	dolphins	laughs	smart
beach	don't	ocean	stupid
buy	embarrassed	push	trouble
cat	hates	save	understand
do	humans	sensitive	zillion

Jennifer: Cats are very _____*sensitive*_____. You know, sometimes when a
                                    1
_____ does something kind of _____—I don't
              2   3
know, falls off a table or something—and everybody _____?
                                                         4
You can just tell that the cat feels really _____. It
                                              5
_____ to be laughed at.
       6

Conversational Listening Practice Featured in Part Two
In **Part Two,** students are given a chance to hear authentic conversational language on topics relevant to their interests and everyday concerns. In addition, these listening passages are available in both audio and video formats providing students with the opportunity to study the types of nonverbal cues that accompany oral messages. (page 96)

Part Three: Focus on the Mechanics of Listening and Speaking

Part Three is devoted to providing students with listening and speaking skills that focus on intonation, stress, pronunciation, and various language functions. Here, students learn about the language function of responding to a negative question, and the pronunciation tip focuses on understanding words that are typically reduced in the flow of speech. (pages 101 and 104)

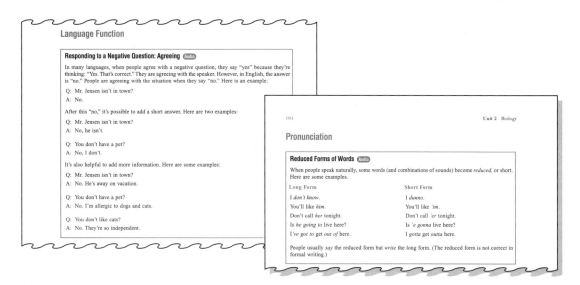

Language Function

Responding to a Negative Question: Agreeing (Audio)

In many languages, when people agree with a negative question, they say "yes" because they're thinking: "Yes. That's correct." They are agreeing with the speaker. However, in English, the answer is "no." People are agreeing with the situation when they say "no." Here is an example:

Q: Mr. Jensen isn't in town?
A: No.

After this "no," it's possible to add a short answer. Here are two examples:

Q: Mr. Jensen isn't in town?
A: No, he isn't.

Q: You don't have a pet?
A: No, I don't.

It's also helpful to add more information. Here are some examples:

Q: Mr. Jensen isn't in town?
A: No. He's away on vacation.

Q: You don't have a pet?
A: No. I'm allergic to dogs and cats.

Q: You don't like cats?
A: No. They're so independent.

104   Unit 2 Biology

Pronunciation

Reduced Forms of Words (Audio)

When people speak naturally, some words (and combinations of sounds) become *reduced*, or short. Here are some examples.

Long Form	Short Form
I *don't know*.	I *dunno*.
You'll like *him*.	You'll like *'im*.
Don't call *her* tonight.	Don't call *'er* tonight.
Is *he going to* live here?	Is *'e gonna* live here?
I've *got to* get *out of* here.	I *gotta* get *outta* here.

People usually *say* the reduced form but *write* the long form. (The reduced form is not correct in formal writing.)

Authentic Broadcast English Featured in Part Four

The listening activities found in **Part Four** of each chapter are all authentic radio segments taken from a variety of sources. In this example, students hear a radio interview with Penny Patterson on National Public Radio. The pages in this section where the listening activities appear, include a shaded bar to indicate that the activities can be done in the language laboratory, at home, or in the classroom. (pages 106 and 108)

106   Unit 2 Biology

.ıːː¦¦ Part Four Broadcast English: Gorilla Love

Before Listening

Koko with her human handler, Penny Patterson   Koko with her pet kitten

Listening

A. Listening for the Main Idea. (Audio) You're going to hear a radio interview with Penny Patterson. Listen for the answer to this question:

• How did people at the Gorilla Foundation find a mate for Koko?

C. Listening for Details. (Audio) Listen to another part of the interview. Then circle the answer to each question.

Ndume

1. Why did the people at the Gorilla Foundation show Koko videos of male gorillas?

   a. Because gorillas enjoy TV, and the humans wanted to make her happy.

   b. Because the humans wanted to find a good mate for her, and female gorillas don't like all male gorillas.

   c. Because female gorillas are shy with other gorillas, and the humans wanted Koko to feel comfortable with "strangers."

2. What was her reaction (response) to the video of a male in Tacoma, Washington?

   a. She loved him.

   b. She hated him.

   c. Her reaction was somewhere between love and hate.

3. How did she react to the video of a male gorilla in an Italian zoo?

   a. She loved him.

   b. She hated him.

   c. Her reaction was somewhere between love and hate.

4. How did she react to Ndume?

   a. She loved him.

   b. She hated him.

   c. Her reaction was somewhere between love and hate.

Abundance of Practice Material

All listening sections in *Quest* are accompanied by a variety of activities that provide students with practice opportunities to complete before, during, and after hearing the passage. In these examples, students gain practice in such skills as listening for details and guessing meaning from context. (pages 109 and 110)

---

110   Unit 2   Biology

D. Guessing Meaning from Context. (Audio) Listen to these sentences. You will hear them in two short pieces from the radio interview. What does each sentence mean? Write your guess.

1. The chemistry isn't there. = _____

_____

2. She went for him. = _____

_____

Chapter Three   Animal Behavior   111

. . : : ¦ ¦ Part Five   Academic English: Do Animals Have Emotions?

Before Listening

 listening **Strategy**

Predicting

Before you listen to a lecture, think about the topic for a few minutes. Do you have any ideas or opinions about this topic? While you listen to the lecture, ask yourself: Are my ideas right or wrong? This will make you an active listener.

A. Predicting. (Pair) You're going to hear a lecture called "Do Animals Have Emotions?" To prepare for the lecture, answer these questions.

1. What do scientists probably say about animals and emotions? Do they think that animals have emotions?

2. Look at these pictures and read the information. In your opinion, why do these animals do these actions?

An otter. Otters will slide down a hill into the water, climb back to the top of the hill, and slide down again and again.

An Australian galah. Galahs will slide down, fly back to the top, and then slide dow[n]

Strategy Boxes Sharpen Students' Skills

Listening Strategy and Speaking Strategy boxes occur frequently throughout each chapter, providing students with practical skills that they can use immediately as they work on the different listening passages. These strategy boxes are always followed by practice activities that allow students to master the strategy at hand. (pages 111 and 112)

---

speaking **Strategy**

Using Nonverbal Communication

When we communicate, we don't always use words. We sometimes "speak" without words. We often express meaning through *nonverbal communication*—in other words, communication with hands, face, and body. (*Nonverbal* means "without words.")

• **Body language** = the way that people move (for communication)

• **Hand gestures** = specific body language that uses the hands for communication

• **Facial expressions** = specific body language that uses the face for communication

(Note: Turn back to page 99. Notice the facial expressions.)

Listening

A. Listening for the Main Idea. (Audio) Listen to the lecture. As you listen, follow the outline on pages 114–115, but don't write yet. Just try to answer this question:

- What do scientists believe about animals and emotions?

B. Finding Examples. (Audio) Listen to these short sections from the lecture and answer the questions.

1. What is an example of a domestic animal that appears to have emotions?

   Animal: _____

   Action: _____

   Emotion: _____

2. What are examples of two animals that appear to do some things for fun?

   Example 1: _____

   Example 2: _____

3. What is an example of a sound that "goes with" emotion?

   Example: _____

4. What are examples of animals that are close to humans?

   Example 1: _____

   Example 2: _____

Listening Focus in Part Five: Authentic Academic Lectures

The listening passages in each chapter of *Quest* increase in length and complexity, and culminate with an academic lecture in **Part Five.** These lectures were written by content experts in each subject area and adapted to meet the special needs of English language students. A variety of activities accompany each lecture. In this example, students learn how to listen for the main idea and examples. The lecture in this chapter, *Do Animals Have Emotions?*, was written by biologist Stem Wilcox. (pages 113 and 114)

Emphasis on Note-Taking Skills

Quest offers intensive note-taking practice to accompany each lecture in **Part Five.** Students are provided with structured outlines to assist them in taking accurate notes. Moreover, well-organized postlistening activities teach students how to use and refer to their notes in order to answer both general and specific questions about the lecture. (pages 114 and 116)

C. Taking Notes. (Audio) Listen to the lecture again. This time fill in the outline.

Do Animals Have Emotions?

I. Introduction: Animals that seem to express emotion

  A. Domestic animals

    1. _____

      a. Happy: wag tail

      b. Sad

        Example: dog mourned when friend died

    2. Cats

    3. Horses

  B. Wild animals at play

    1. Otters

    2. _____

    3. _____

After Listening

A. Using Your Notes. (Pair) Use your notes to discuss these questions about the lecture.

1. What do scientists believe about animals and emotions?

2. Why do otters slide down to the water (and parrots slide down a wire) again and again?

3. Why aren't there many studies of emotions in animals?

4. What is a possible solution—a way to study emotions in animals?

Chapter Three Animal Behavior   117

🎓 *academic* Strategy

Understanding a Speaker's Point of View

Sometimes a speaker tells you his or her point of view (way of looking at something). The speaker doesn't say his or her opinion directly, but you can guess it.

Example: Most of us who have been around domestic dogs, cats, and horses think that these
               animals have emotions.

The speaker uses the pronoun *us.* The speaker includes himself in the group of people with this opinion about animals: Animals have emotions.
          Sometimes you can guess a speaker's point of view. You can look for words that give you clues.

Practice. Here is a sentence from the lecture. Read it and answer the questions.
          Another very cute example of play behavior is from the Australian galahs. They slide
          down a wire.

1. Does the speaker think that animals can play? Explain your answer. _____

   _____

2. Does the speaker enjoy watching animals? Explain your answer. _____

   _____

Academic Strategy Boxes
Found in each chapter, these strategy boxes prepare students to be active participants in the academic environment. In this example, students are given instruction in how to understand a speaker's point of view. (page 117)

🔺 *Step* Beyond

In this activity, you'll study nonverbal communication.

A. Doing Research

Step One

Choose *one* of these situations for a homework project.

• Watch gorillas or chimpanzees. (You can go to a zoo or rent a nature video.)
• Watch humans. (Choose a place where you can see a lot of nonverbal communication—maybe a
  shopping center or public park.)
• Watch humans from a different culture. (You can watch people at an international school, at an
  international festival, or in a foreign film.)
• Watch a TV program with the sound on *mute* (silent).

**Step Beyond: Chapter-Culminating
Speaking Activities**
Each chapter ends with a *Step Beyond* speaking activity. The content of this activity takes the form of a presentation, a debate, a survey, or an interview. It is based on the chapter's theme and incorporates the listening and speaking skills that students have practiced in previous sections. In this example, students first do research on a topic of their choice and then report their results in groups using a chart. (pages 117 and 118)

118   Unit 2 Biology

Step Two

Watch your situation for 30 minutes. As you watch, pay attention to body language, hand gestures, and facial expressions. In Column 1 of the chart on this page, record everything that you notice.

Step Three

Try to interpret your notes. In your opinion, what is the meaning of this nonverbal communication? Put this in Column 2.

Example:

Column 1	Column 2
One man hits another on the back. Both are smiling.	Congratulations? You did a good job?

B. Reporting Results. In small groups, talk about your project. What did you learn about the nonverbal communication in your situation? How much could you understand without words? Find students with the same situation as yours. How do your ideas compare?

Nonverbal Communication

Column 1	Column 2
• Body Language • Hand Gestures • Facial Expressions	What Does It Mean?

summary of Listening and Speaking Skills

Chapter	Listening/Speaking Strategies	Mechanics/Academic Strategies
Getting Started	• taking lecture notes • finding practice opportunities • understanding the intonation of tag questions • listening for the main idea • understanding fast or difficult English • talking about your major • making small talk • using tag questions	
1	• guessing meaning from context • understanding numbers • listening for details • taking lecture notes • comparing values • giving advice • planning ahead	• asking for and giving directions • understanding interjections • the *th* sound understanding higher education in the United States
2	• brainstorming • listening for supporting information • guessing meaning from context • making eye contact • outlining (for a presentation)	• starting a conversation • continuing a conversation • reduced forms of words • *wh-* questions asking questions
3	• listening for stressed words • understanding emotion from tone of voice • making predictions • listening for examples • using nonverbal communication	• statements and questions • responding to a negative question • reduced forms of words understanding a speaker's point of view

(Continued)

Chapter	Listening/Speaking Strategies	Mechanics/Academic Strategies
4	• listening for reasons • listening for numerical information • knowing when important information is coming • taking turns	• asking for clarification • offering clarification • emphasis for clarification • reduced forms in questions with *Do* <u>asking questions before listening</u> <u>comparing information</u>
5	• thinking ahead to prepare for listening • being prepared for an important explanation • listening for examples in groups • listening for dates • getting feedback	• introducing yourself to someone who doesn't remember you • responding to an introduction • identifying yourself on the phone • pronunciation: /ɪ/ vs. /i/ <u>working cooperatively</u>
6	• taking lecture notes • talking about symbols • saying something in a different way	• agreeing and disagreeing • showing you don't really agree • pronunciation: verbs ending in *-ed* • giving an opinion <u>understanding irony</u> <u>synthesizing information</u>

introduction

Getting Started

This chapter will get you started with the material in this book. You will also listen to and discuss basic information about college life.

Introduction to Academic Life

The time to prepare for college is *now*. It's never too soon. You're already taking a big step. You're improving your English. Students who plan to go to college in the United States or Canada also need to know something about the system of higher education in those countries. What can you expect? What do you need to do?

Practice 1. **Audio**   Read along as you listen to the speaker explain some of the basics of college life. You'll hear the passage a second time, but don't read along that time.

College in the United States and Canada: Part One

Many students begin at a four-year college or university. Many others begin their first year (the **freshman** year) at a two-year **community college.** After their second year (the **sophomore** year), students get a certificate from the community college. Many students transfer to a four-year school for their third (**jun-**
5 **ior**) and fourth (**senior**) years.

In the first four years of college, students are **undergraduates.** When they graduate, they receive a **degree**—probably a B. A. (Bachelor of Arts) or B. S. (Bachelor of Science).

Students who continue their studies after graduation are in **graduate school.**
10 For short, we call this **"grad school."** They are **"grad students."** They are in a master's program. After two more years, they may receive a **master's degree**—perhaps an M. A. (Master of Arts), M. S. (Master of Science), M. B. A. (Master of Business Administration), or M. F. A. (Master of Fine Art). Some students continue a get a **doctor of philosophy** degree (Ph.D.). This is the highest university degree.

15 Most colleges are two-year community colleges. Some are four-year schools. Perhaps it's important to note the difference between **college** and **university.** Both are kinds of higher education. Both are after high school. But a university is never a two-year school (such as a community college). Also, a university has a graduate school. In Canada, students say "I'm in college" or "I'm in university." But in the
20 United States, undergraduate students usually just say "I'm in college." This might really mean "college," or it might mean "university." The meaning is not clear. Graduate students usually say "I'm in grad school."

listening Strategy

Taking Lecture Notes

It's important for college students to take good notes during a **lecture**—a professor's speech or talk. A lot of the material on an exam probably comes from the lectures in a class. Information in class lectures is often different from information in the textbook for a class. You'll practice taking lecture notes in every chapter of this book. Here are some suggestions.

• Take notes. Don't "just listen." You won't remember the information later.

• Don't try to write *everything*. Note taking is not dictation. If you try to write every word, you might not catch important points in the lecture.

• Write all important information. How do you know that it's important? Your professor might do the following:

  ✓ Tell you that it's important

  ✓ Emphasize it (say it loudly and clearly)

  ✓ Say it more than one time

  ✓ Write it on the board

  ✓ Give a **definition**

    Definitions of new words are usually important. A definition is the meaning of a word. Sometimes your professor will say "X means Y." But more often the professor will say "X is Y" or "Xs are Ys." Very often the professor gives a **synonym** (a word with the same meaning) or a definition right after the new word.

Examples: *University* basically means <u>a college that includes a grad school</u>.

         A *university* is <u>a college that includes a grad school</u>.

         A *university*, <u>a college that includes a grad school</u>, is one form of higher education.

Practice 2. Here is an example of one student's lecture notes. Look back at Part One of the passage "College in the United States and Canada," on page 2. Compare the lecture and the notes. What is in the notes? What *isn't* in the notes?

College in the U.S. and Canada

I. Undergraduate Students

    A. Years

        1. Freshman (1st year) {2-year community college or 4-year school}

        2. Sophomore (2nd)

        3. Junior (3rd)

        4. Senior (4th)

    B. Graduate/receive a Degree

        1. B.A.

        2. B.S.

II. Graduate School (= grad school)

    A. Grad students—in a master's program or Ph.D. program

    B. Receive a master's degree (after 2 years)

        1. M.A.

        2. M.S.

        3. M.B.A.

        4. M.F.A.

    C. Receive a Ph.D.

III. Definitions: <u>College</u> and <u>University</u>

    A. Both after high school

    B. University

        1. Never just 2 years

        2. Has a grad school

    C. Canada: "I'm in college."/"I'm in university."

    D. U.S.: "I'm in college" = <u>college</u> or <u>university</u> (!!)

Practice 3. **Audio** Listen to Part Two of the lecture. This time take notes: fill in the blanks on the outline. This will be the important information. Pay special attention to definitions. If necessary, listen to the lecture more than one time.

College in the United States and Canada: Part Two

   I. General Education Requirements (U.S. only)
     A. Definition: _____

       _____

     B. Examples: _____

       _____

  II. Electives
     A. Definition: _____

       _____

     B. Good idea to: _____

       _____

 III. Major
     A. Definition: _____

       _____

     B. Freshman and sophomore years: _____

       _____

     C. Junior and senior years: _____

       _____

speaking Strategy

Talking about Your Major

The word *major* can be a noun.

Examples: This is Evan.

His **major** is broadcast journalism.

Her name is Chrissy.

Her **major** is going to be psychology.

Major is also a verb. You can **major in** a subject.

Examples: His name is Brandon.

He's **majoring in*** computer science.

This is Tanya.

She's **going to major in** business.

* Notice the preposition *in*.

To ask about majors, you can say

- What's your major?
- What are you going to major in?
- What do you think you'll major in?

To answer, you can say

- My major is . . .
- I'm going to major in . . .
- I think I'll major in . . .
- I'm planning to major in . . .
- I might major in . . .
- I'm not sure yet.
- I'm undecided.

Practice 4. Walk around the classroom with your book and a pencil. Ask ten students about their majors and fill in the chart.

Note: This is a good time to learn your classmates' first names. After they tell you their name, be sure to ask about spelling.

Example: A: Hi. What's your name?

B: Klarissa.

A: How do you spell that?

B: K-L-A-R-I-S-S-A.

A: Klarissa. OK, thanks.

Name	Major	Name	Major
1.		6.	
2.		7.	
3.		8.	
4.		9.	
5.		10.	

Introduction to Listening and Speaking

In the listening activities in this book, you'll hear three types of English in each chapter:

- Conversations
- Radio broadcasts
- College (or university) lectures

You'll also practice speaking in different situations:

- Talking with a partner and in small groups
- Collecting information from many students
- Giving presentations

This is a lot of practice in listening and speaking, *but it isn't enough.* To learn English fast—and well— you need to practice outside of class.

listening Strategy

Finding Practice Opportunities

Where can you practice listening to English? Here are just a few suggestions.

- Every day listen to five minutes of the news (in English) on the radio. If possible, tape this. Listen to it over and over.

- Choose a few TV programs in English. Watch these same programs every week.

- Do you have a VCR? Tape your favorite English-language program once a week. Watch part of it over and over.

- Rent movies in English.

- Find a computer website with listening activities. Listen to it regularly. Examples are Dave's Cafe <http://www.eslcafe.com> and Randall's ESL Cyber Listening Lab <http://esl-lab.com>.

speaking Strategy

Finding Practice Opportunities

Where can you practice speaking English? Here are just a few suggestions.

- After class, go for coffee with a classmate who doesn't speak your language.

- Find an English-speaking student who is studying your language. Meet once a week. Practice 30 minutes in your language and 30 minutes in English.

- Volunteer at a hospital or homeless shelter.

- Make small talk with strangers in public places.

Practice 1. **Group**   With two or three other students, discuss this question: What are other places where you can practice English outside of class? Make a list. After you finish, each group will report at least one place to the class. (Your teacher might put your suggestions on a list on the bulletin board.)

_____   _____

_____   _____

_____   _____

_____   _____

speaking Strategy

Making Small Talk

Small talk is a very short conversation about things that are not very important. Often two strangers make small talk. They have short conversations of two sentences. In the first sentence, one person usually talks about the immediate situation (what's happening around you). This sentence often ends with a **tag question.** In the second sentence, the other person gives a **reply**—an answer.

Example: A: It's cold today, isn't it?

B: Yes, it is.

Small talk is never about very important subjects. It can be about the weather, sports, the time, a product in the market, and so on. It is a way to be friendly. (And it is one way to practice a new language!)

In many English-speaking countries, strangers sometimes make small talk. Here are some situations for small talk: at a bus stop, waiting in line, at a party, in a supermarket, in the school cafeteria, at a music festival, and so on. Small talk seems to be less common in large cities and more common in smaller towns. Some observers say that small talk is less common in England than in other English-speaking countries, including the United States, Canada, and Australia. In all of these countries (even England), there is usually a lot of small talk in a crisis. A "crisis situation" might be a very late bus or a train that breaks down.

Of course, it's necessary to be a little careful. Choose "safe" people to speak to. For example, it's not a good idea to make small talk late at night with strangers on a dark street!

Practice 2. Group   Discuss the answers to these questions. Then report your answers to the class.

1. In your country, do people sometimes make small talk with strangers?

2. If so, what do they talk about?

3. If not, why?

4. What are good situations for small talk? What are bad situations for small talk?

5. What do you think about making small talk with strangers?

speaking **Strategy**

Using Tag Questions

In a tag question, a "tag" at the end of a statement makes it into a question.

Affirmative Statement	**Negative Tag**
It's cold today,	isn't it?
She's the foreign student advisor,	isn't she?
These are expensive,	aren't they?
We had Chapter Three for homework,	didn't we?
The oranges look good,	don't they?
The professor speaks fast,	doesn't she?

Negative Statement	**Affirmative Tag**
This isn't ready,	is it?
He hasn't done it yet,	has he?
You don't have one,	do you?
You didn't take Business 101,	did you?
There aren't any lab fees,	are there?
The students weren't in the lab,	were they?

As you see, for an affirmative statement, the tag is *negative*. For a negative statement, the tag is *affirmative*.

Practice 3.   Write the correct tag to complete each sentence.

1. They're busy, _____?

2. This bus goes to Brand Street, _____?

3. It was a great movie, _____?

4. This bus doesn't go to Riverside, _____?

5. The biology books are over there, _____?

6. The history department isn't offering History 207 this term, _____?

7. The test wasn't very hard, _____?

8. The homework was interesting, _____?

9. We didn't have to do Chapter Five, _____?

10. The food at this party is fabulous, _____?

listening Strategy

Understanding the Intonation of Tag Questions Audio

If you really need information (and if you really aren't sure about the answer), your voice goes *up* on a tag question. It's a real question.

Example: They're busy, aren't they?

(= I'm not sure. Are they busy?)

If you know the answer (and are just making small talk), your voice goes *down*.

Example: They're busy, aren't they?

(= I know that they are busy.)

Practice 4. Audio   Now listen to the ten sentences from Practice 3. Are they "real" questions? (Does the speaker really need information?) Check (✓) *yes* or *no*. When you finish, listen again. Repeat each sentence after the speaker.

	Yes	No			Yes	No
1.	_____	_____		6.	_____	_____
2.	_____	_____		7.	_____	_____
3.	_____	_____		8.	_____	_____
4.	_____	_____		9.	_____	_____
5.	_____	_____		10.	_____	_____

Practice 5. Video/Audio   Listen to these five examples. Is the first person really asking for information? Or is this just small talk? Check (✓) *Real Question* or *Small Talk*. If necessary, listen several times.

	Real Question	Small Talk
1.	_____	_____
2.	_____	_____
3.	_____	_____
4.	_____	_____
5.	_____	_____

Practice 6. (Pair) Make small talk in these situations. Take turns playing the roles of Student A and Student B. Follow the directions in the boxes.

Example: **Situation for Student A:** You're choosing classes for the new term.

You think that English 101 is a required class, but you aren't sure.

Situation for Student B: You're choosing classes for the new term.

English 101 is a required class.

Small talk: A: We have to take English 101, don't we?

B: Yeah, we do.

Student A

Start a conversation with your partner. Use a tag question in each situation. (If you need information, make sure that your voice goes up. If you know the answer, make sure that your voice goes down.)

Situation 1.   You're taking a tour of Valley College. It's a nice campus.

Situation 2.   You're in the school cafeteria. The soup looks good.

Situation 3.   You're in your history class. The homework last night was really hard.

Situation 4.   You're in the school bookstore. You need to buy a book for your math class, but there aren't any.

Situation 5.   You're at a new coffee shop. You're trying something called Iced Vanilla Mocha Coffee. It's delicious.

Situation 6.   You're coming out of a movie theater. The movie was sad.

Situation 7.   You're coming out of your English class. You don't think that the teacher gave you any homework, but you aren't sure.

Situation 8.   You're in a computer store. You see a great new computer game, but it's expensive.

Situation 9.   You're on your way to the library. You think it's closed on Sunday, but you aren't sure.

Situation 10.   It's a very, very hot summer day. You walk into a cool building.

Student B

Make small talk with your partner. If your partner asks a "real" question, you can use any information below, or you can make up an answer.

Situation 1. You're taking a tour of Valley College.

Situation 2. You're in the school cafeteria.

Situation 3. You're in your history class.

Situation 4. You're in the school bookstore. There aren't any books for a math class. The book is **out of stock.**

Situation 5. You're at a new coffee shop. You're trying something called Iced Vanilla Mocha Coffee.

Situation 6. You're coming out of a movie theater.

Situation 7. You're coming out of your English class. The teacher didn't give any homework.

Situation 8. You're in a computer store. You see a computer game. It's very expensive.

Situation 9. You're on campus. It's a Sunday. The library isn't open on Sunday.

Situation 10. It's a very, very hot summer day. You're inside a cool building.

 listening **Strategy**

Listening for the Main Idea

You don't always understand everything when people speak. Sometimes 90 percent of their words are impossible to understand! But if the main idea is in the other 10 percent, then you understand the important information. That's good! The main idea *is* the important information. The other words are not as necessary.

How can you find the main idea? Here are some suggestions.

- Sometimes a speaker basically tells you, "This is the main idea." The speaker might say the following:

    ✓ My point is . . .

    ✓ What I mean is . . .

    ✓ The idea is that . . .

- Sometimes the person speaks more slowly, loudly, and carefully for the main idea.

- The main idea is *not* a detail (a small point). It's not an example. (Examples usually come *after* the main idea.)

- The main idea is often at the beginning or end of a group of sentences.

- The main idea is sometimes the answer to an important question.

Practice 7. **Audio**   Listen to this piece from a radio call-in program. (On this kind of program, people call in and give their opinion on the radio.) This program is about college. The caller answers the question: What advice can you give new college students? Listen for his answer. The answer is the main idea. Circle the answer. If necessary, listen several times.

    Daniel says that it's good for students to

a. Enter college

b. Listen to their parents

c. Study what they like

d. Be excited about leaving home

listening Strategy

Understanding Fast or Difficult English

Many people speak fast or use difficult vocabulary. You can't understand everything. What can you do? Here are some suggestions.

* Don't be shy. Ask the person to repeat. Say one of the following:

   ✓ Excuse me?

   ✓ Could you repeat that?

   ✓ What was that again?

* Practice with the radio. Tape a short piece. Listen over and over. Soon it will seem slower.

* Don't worry about every word.

* Listen for the main idea and *important* details.

* Have questions in mind as you listen.

Practice 8. **Audio**   Listen to the next speaker, a guest on the same radio program. He speaks fast. How much can you understand? First, read these seven sentences. Then listen to the tape. Check (✓) *True* or *False*. If necessary, listen several times.

	True	False
1. The speaker agrees with Daniel.	_____	_____
2. The young woman in the story was majoring in business.	_____	_____
3. She enjoyed her major.	_____	_____
4. She wanted to major in dance.	_____	_____
5. She could make a lot of money as a dancer.	_____	_____
6. She gave up her dreams.	_____	_____
7. The speaker thinks that the woman's story is sad.	_____	_____

Practice 9. **Group**   Discuss these questions. Compare your ideas. Then report your group's answers to the class.

1. Which is better?

  • To major in something that you love

  • To major in something that will get you a good job

2. Is there a "perfect" major?

unit

1

Business

chapter One

Career Planning

In this chapter, you'll listen to and discuss advice for new college students. Also, you'll learn about many different college services.

Part One Introduction: Education and Career Success

Students receiving degrees

A. Thinking Ahead. Pair Discuss the answers to these questions.

1. How many students in your country study at a college or at a university after high school: 5 percent (%)? 10 percent? 50 percent? 80 percent?

2. In your country, does a college education help a person to be successful in life?

3. What does *success* mean to you? (Does it mean money? Love? Happiness?)

B. Reading Tables.   Read the tables from the U.S. Census Bureau. As you read, try to answer this question:

- How does education influence a person's income (salary, pay)?

Earnings by Educational Level

Educational Level	Average Annual Salary
Doctorate (Ph.D.)	$64,550
Professional*	85,322
Master's degree	47,609
Bachelor's degree	36,980
Community college	27,780
Some college, no degree	22,392
High school	21,431
Not a high school graduate	14,013
* For example, a lawyer or a doctor	

Source: Census Bureau, *Current Population Survey,* March 1996 Update.

Fields of College/University Degree

In Order of Monthly Earnings (high to low)

1. Medicine/dentistry
2. Law
3. Economics
4. Engineering
5. Agriculture/forestry
6. Mathematics/statistics
7. Business/management
8. Physical/earth sciences
9. English/journalism
10. Psychology
11. Police science/law enforcement
12. Biology
13. Social sciences
14. Religion/theology
15. Nursing/pharmacy/health
16. Education
17. Liberal arts/humanities
18. Vocational/technical studies
19. Home economics

Source: Census Bureau, *Current Population Reports,* December 1995.

C. Discussing Tables. Pair Discuss your opinions.

1. Are you surprised by anything on these two tables? If so, what? Why?

2. In your country, are such lists similar or different? (In which fields do people with a college/university degree make a lot of money? In which fields do people with a college/university degree not make a lot of money?)

D. Ranking Values.   Look at this list. What is important to *your* happiness? Rank the things (1 = the most important; 2 = the next important, etc.).

_____ family life   _____ income (money)   _____ work

_____ friends   _____ love life   _____ your children's education

_____ health   _____ quality of life

(When you finish, turn to page 53 to see how Americans, Japanese, and Europeans answered this.)

speaking Strategy

Comparing Values

Here are some ways to compare values.

Questions: • What's most important to you?

               • Is X more important to you than Y?

               • Why is X more important to you?

Statements: • To me, the most important thing in life is X.

               • X is much more important to me than Y.

               • To me, X and Y are equally important.

               • X is important to me because . . .

E. Discussing Values. **Group**   Compare your answers to Exercise D with those of other students.

F. Journal Writing.   In this book, you are going to keep a journal. In your journal, you are going to do freewriting activities. In freewriting, you write quickly about what you are thinking or feeling. Grammar and form are not very important in freewriting. Your ideas and thoughts are important. You will have a time limit of five minutes for your journal writing in this book. You can buy a special notebook for your journal, or you can write your ideas on separate pieces of paper and keep them in a binder or folder.

    Choose *one* of these topics. Write about it for five minutes. Don't worry about grammar and don't use a dictionary. Just put as many ideas as you can on paper.

• What is important to your happiness (and why)?

• Can education make you happier?

• Is a college education necessary for your work or your career choice?

Part Two Everyday English: College for Beginners

Before Listening

speaking Strategy

Giving Advice

Here are three ways to give advice.

	Affirmative	Negative
Command	Study hard.	Don't study too hard.
Should	You should study hard.	You shouldn't study too hard.
Be sure to . . .	Be sure to study hard.	Be sure not to study too hard.

A. Thinking Ahead.   What advice can you give to students who are starting high school? (Help them to learn from your experience!) Write a list of "dos" (affirmative advice) and "don'ts" (negative advice).

Dos	Don'ts

B. Comparing Ideas. (Group)   Share your lists from Exercise A. Was there any piece of advice on everyone's list? Report one piece of advice from your group to the class.

C. Predicting. (Group)   You're going to listen to eleven people. They give advice to students who are starting college (university) in the United States. What will they say? In small groups, make predictions. Make a list.

_____   _____

_____   _____

_____   _____

Listening

A. Listening for the Main Idea. (Video/Audio)   Listen to the opinions of these eleven people. Don't worry about new words or fast English. As you listen, try to answer this question:

• What advice do *most* of the people give—to work hard (especially study hard) or do something else (some other thing)?

B. Listening for Details. (Video/Audio)   Now listen again. What advice does each person give? Put check marks (✓) in the boxes.

Person Number	Work/Study Hard	Enjoy Yourself/Have Fun	Something Else
1			✓
2			
3			
4			
5			
6			
7			
8			
9			
10			
11			

 listening Strategy

Guessing Meaning from Context (Audio)

You usually won't understand everything in a conversation in English. There will be new words. Of course, you can't stop a conversation to use a dictionary. But you can often **guess meaning from context.** This means that the context (other words *around* the new word) can often help you with meaning. How can you use the context? *Listen for words that mean the same as the new word. People often repeat the same thing in different ways.*

Examples: My brother **dropped out** of business school. Our parents weren't happy that he quit, but he never really liked business.

(Here you see that **dropped out** means "quit.")

The **majority** of college students are now women. They are more than half of the student population.

(Here you see that **majority** means "more than half.")

In addition, it's important to focus (or concentrate) on things that you *understand*. Don't focus on things that you *don't* understand.

C. Vocabulary: Guessing Meaning from Context. Video/Audio Listen again to three of the people. They use the following words and expressions. What do they mean? Guess from the context. Write the meanings. Don't use a dictionary.

1. silly = _____

2. apply yourself = _____

3. Don't get sucked in by social pressures. = _____

D. Listening for Specific Ideas. Video/Audio Listen again to these people. Write your answer to each question.

1. *Person 1:* Why should students ask questions?

   _____

   _____

2. *Person 2:* How much time should students spend on homework?

   _____

3. *Person 5:* Person 5 says "Be more open-minded." How can students be more open-minded, in her opinion?

   _____

   _____

4. *Person 9:* What shouldn't students worry about? Why?

   _____

   _____

After Listening

A. Discussion. Pair Discuss the answers to these questions.

1. Were you surprised by any advice that you heard? If so, what surprised you?

2. Was any advice the same as your predictions on page 24?

3. In your own country, what advice would people give to new college students?

speaking Strategy

Planning Ahead

One speaker advised students ". . . not to be afraid to ask questions." But sometimes it's difficult to ask questions in a new language. Here is a suggestion.

Step One: Imagine situations where you will need help.

Step Two: Plan and practice questions in these situations *before you need to ask.*

Also, remember this: Most people like to help, so don't be shy.

B. Planning Ahead: Making Questions. What is a good question for each of these answers? (Don't use any of the underlined words in your questions.)

1. Question: _____?

   Answer: I'm <u>fine</u>, thanks.

2. Question: _____?

   Answer: His name is <u>Dr. Levi</u>.

3. Question: _____?

   Answer: The library is open <u>from 8:00 A.M. to 9:00 P.M.</u>

4. Question: _____?

   Answer: We have to read <u>Chapter Five</u>.

5. Question: _____?

   Answer: The class meets <u>on Tuesday and Thursday.</u>

6. Question: _____?

   Answer: <u>Yes</u>, the test was <u>really</u> hard.

7. Question: _____?

   Answer: T. A. means "<u>teaching assistant</u>."

8. Question: _____?

   Answer: <u>No</u>, it is<u>n't</u> far.

9. Question: _____?

Answer: The Counseling Center is <u>in Edison Hall, next to the Admissions Office</u>.

10. Question: _____?

Answer: <u>Go down one block and turn left.</u> The Copy Center is right there.

C. Practice. **Pair** Now practice your ten questions with a partner. Take turns. Ask and answer questions. Be sure to thank your partner for the information.

D. Asking the Right Questions.   What can you ask in these situations? First, write your questions. Then compare your questions with those of another student.

Situations

1. You meet the secretary in the English Department. She tells you her name, but you don't hear her clearly. What can you ask her?

Question: _____

2. You're in the college library. You don't know how to use the computer catalog to find a book. What can you ask the librarian?

Question: _____

3. You want a job on campus (= at the college). You go to the Career Planning and Placement Office, but you don't know how to apply for a job. How can you ask the person at the desk (or counter) for advice?

Question: _____

4. You're confused about your major. You want to study something that you love. You also want a good job when you graduate. You need an appointment with a career counselor. What can you ask at the Career Planning and Placement Office?

Question: _____

5. It's the first day of your history class. It meets on Monday, Wednesday, and Friday. The professor tells the class, "Your discussion section will meet on Thursdays at ten o'clock." You don't understand *discussion section*. What can you ask another student?

   Question: _____

6. On the first day of class, a student next to you tells you, "I've heard that the T. A. for this class is really good." You don't understand *T. A.* What can you ask the student?

   Question: _____

7. You're in class. You were absent yesterday. You want to know what happened in class. What can you ask the student next to you?

   Question: _____

8. You're in the college cafeteria. You want to get the soup, but you don't eat meat. You worry that there is meat in the soup. What can you ask a cafeteria worker?

   Question: _____

9. You're new at this school, and you're a little lost. You also need some cash. You want to find an ATM (automatic teller machine). What can you ask a student?

   Question: _____

10. You're near school. You need to find a copy store because you need to copy your composition. You don't know this neighborhood well. What can you ask a stranger on the street?

   Question: _____

E. Getting Information for Yourself.   Group   What confuses you about your class, school, neighborhood, or city? Write your own questions. Then, in small groups, share your questions. Can any of your classmates answer them?

Examples: Where do I go to get information on part-time jobs?

   What are some good cheap places to eat near school?

. : : : : : **Part Three** The Mechanics of Listening
and Speaking

Language Functions

> ### Asking for and Giving Directions (Audio)
>
> Here are several ways to ask a stranger for directions. (You can use either *can* or *could* in questions like these.)
>
> - Excuse me. Could you tell me where to find an ATM?
> - Excuse me. Can you tell me where to find an ATM?
> - Can you tell me where an ATM is?
> - Excuse me. Could you tell me how to get to an ATM?
>
> There are many possible answers. Read these conversations as you listen to them on the tape.
>
> A: Excuse me. Could you tell me how to get to the Admissions Office?
> B: Uh-huh. Just go straight and make a left at the corner. It's right there.
> A: Thanks.
> B: No problem.
>
> A: Excuse me. Can you tell me where to find a post office?
> B: Um, sure. There's one across from the park. Go down two blocks and make a right. It's next to an office building.
> A: Thanks a lot.
> B: Uh-huh.

A. Practice. (Audio)   Look at the map on page 31 as you listen to each conversation. Follow the directions. Write the letter of each place in the blank. If necessary, listen to each conversation several times.

_____ **1.** college library   _____ **4.** bank

_____ **2.** drugstore   _____ **5.** career planning office

_____ **3.** bookstore

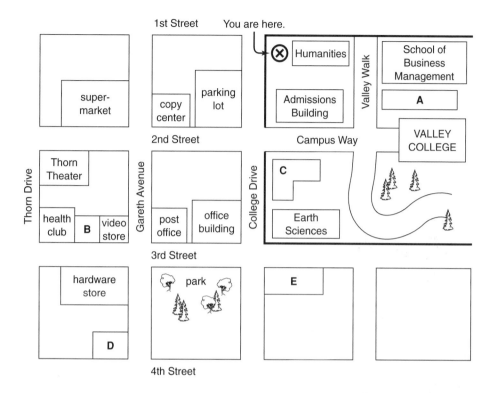

Intonation

Understanding Interjections (Audio)

Several interjections in English are common in conversation. They are informal. Here are some examples.

Interjections	Meanings
Uh-huh.	Yes.
	You're welcome.
Huh?	What? Pardon?
Uh-uh.	No.
Uh . . . /Um . . .	I'm thinking; I'm not sure what to say.
Uh-oh.	I made a mistake.
	There is a problem.

B. Practice. **Audio**   Listen to each conversation. What does the second person mean? Check (✓) the answer.

Conversation	Second Person's Meaning				
	Yes	No	You're Welcome.	What?/Pardon?	There's a Problem!
1					
2					
3					
4					
5					
6					

C. Practice. **Pair**   One of you plays the role of Student A, and the other is Student B. Follow the directions in the boxes.

Example: **Question:** Are you busy?

Answer: Uh-uh.

Student A

• Say each of the following to your partner. Wait for a response.

1. Could I borrow your pencil?
2. Thanks a lot.
3. Are you getting hungry?
4. I think the teacher might surprise us with a big test tomorrow.
5. Have you ever been to Algeria?

• Then respond to your partner's questions and statements. Use one of the interjections on page 31 in your response.

Student B

- Respond to your partner. Use one of the interjections on page 31 in your response.
- Then say each of the following to your partner. Wait for a response.

   1. Do we have any homework tonight?

   2. I can't find my keys anywhere.

   3. Could I borrow your dictionary for a minute?

   4. Thanks.

   5. Do you speak Swahili?

Pronunciation

The *th* Sound **Audio**

The letters *th* can stand for several different sounds. One of these is the sound in <u>thanks</u>. To pronounce the *th* sound, put the tip of your tongue *between* your teeth *just a little* and blow. *Do not stick your tongue between your lips!* Listen to these contrasts.

s	th
sank	thank
sick	thick
saw	thaw
pass	path
tense	tenth

Many ordinal numbers contain the *th* sound at the end. Here are some examples:

fourth (4th)	seventh (7th)	tenth (10th)
fifth (5th)	eighth (8th)	eleventh (11th)
sixth (6th)	ninth (9th	twelfth (12th)

D. Practice. **Audio**   In each pair of words, circle the one that you hear.

1. sank — thank

2. sings — things

3. saw — thaw

4. sick — thick

5. pass — path

6. worse — worth

7. force — fourth

8. sigh — thigh

9. seem — theme

10. tense — tenth

11. eights — eighth

12. some — thumb

E. Practice. (Audio) Look again at the box. Repeat the words after the speaker.

F. Practice. (Audio) Read along as you listen to this short conversation. Then listen again and repeat each sentence after the speaker. Pay special attention to words with *th*.

A: Excuse me. I think I'm lost. I'm looking for Thorn Theater.

B: Oh, it's not far. It's on Thorn Drive, between Ninth and Tenth Street. It's the fourth building from the corner.

A: Thanks a lot.

G. Information Gap. (Pair) Work with a partner. One of you works with the map on this page. The other works with the map on page 218. Don't look at your partner's map. Take turns. Ask and answer questions about the location of buildings. Put letters on your map.

Example: A: Where's Sam's Store?
              B: It's on Gareth Avenue. It's the second building from the corner.

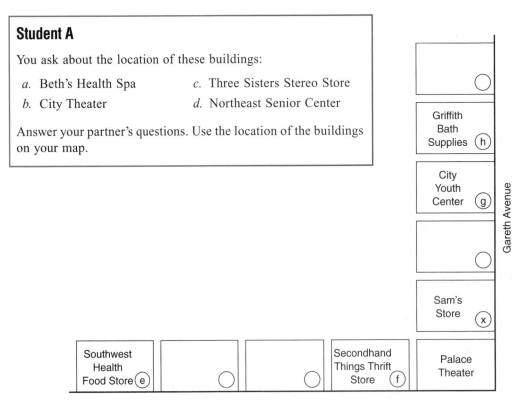

Student A

You ask about the location of these buildings:

a. Beth's Health Spa   c. Three Sisters Stereo Store
b. City Theater   d. Northeast Senior Center

Answer your partner's questions. Use the location of the buildings on your map.

Griffith Bath Supplies (h)

City Youth Center (g)

Sam's Store (x)

Gareth Avenue

Southwest Health Food Store (e)

Secondhand Things Thrift Store (f)

Palace Theater

Tenth Street

Review: Language Functions

Asking for and Giving Directions `Video/Audio`

Listen to these examples. People are asking for and giving directions. The examples will help you to do the next section. (Note: One person does something in the videotape version that is very impolite. Can you find it?)

Put It Together

A. Asking for and Giving Directions. `Pair`   Use the map on page 31 to ask for and give directions. You can look back at the sample conversations on page 30 and use the expressions in this box.

Go down (or up) one/two/three blocks.*	
Turn left/right.	Make a left/right.
Go past the _____.	It's right there.
It's right there on your left/right.	It's across from the _____.
It's on Thorn Drive/Gareth Avenue/Third Street.**	
It's next to the _____.	
It's on the corner of _____ and _____.	
It's in the middle of the block.	

* In English, people count *blocks,* not streets.
** Notice that in English, street names don't have *the* before them.

B. Talking about Your Neighborhood. (Pair)   Do the following activities:

1. Think of two or three places near your school. Then practice asking for and giving directions to these places.

2. Draw a map of the neighborhood around your house. Use it with your partner. Practice asking for and giving directions.

. : : ! ! ! **Part Four** Broadcast English: College Today

Before Listening

A. Thinking Ahead. (Group)   You are going to hear more of the radio program from the Getting Started chapter. The speakers talk about two topics: (1) differences between college today and college 50 years ago and (2) advice to new students. To prepare to listen, answer these questions.

1. In your country, how are colleges today different from colleges 50 years ago? Think about libraries, technology, possible majors, activities, and students. Make a list.

   Example:

50 Years Ago	Today
50 years ago: most students rich	middle class and poor, too

2. In Part Two, you listened to advice on going to college. Now you'll listen to more advice—this time from *experts* (people who know a lot about a subject). What advice do you expect from them? Make a list.

   _____

   _____

   _____

   _____

B. Vocabulary Preparation.   Before you listen, look over this list of words and their meanings. They are from the radio program. Then fill in the blanks with words or expressions from the box.

Words/Expressions	Meanings
higher education	college/university
roughly	approximately/more or less
percent	%
majority	most; more than half
quarters	25-cent coins
appeals to you	you like or enjoy it
joy	great happiness
experimenting	trying new things
dropping out	stopping, leaving school before you finish
of color	black (African American), Asian, American Indian (Native American)
seek out	go and find

1. The _____ of students in that class are Canadian, but some students come from other countries.

2. You should take that class in botany if it _____. It's not a general education requirement, but don't worry about that.

3. The system of _____ in the United States is different from the university system in my country.

4. You should _____ someone in your class to help you.

5. This machine doesn't take dollar bills. It takes only _____.

6. _____ half of the class is majoring in business.

7. She thought about _____ for a year, but her family wants her to graduate soon.

8. I'm thinking of majoring in dance. I always feel such _____ in dance classes! Right now I'm studying Thai dance, and I just love it.

9. Almost thirty _____ of the students can speak more than one language.

10. He's taking classes in biology, acting, Japanese, economics, and history. He's _____ with many subjects, and then he'll decide on a major.

11. About 25 percent of the students are _____, and the rest are white.

academic Strategy

Understanding Higher Education in the United States

Teaching assistants (T. A.s) are graduate students. In addition to their studies, they work part-time at the university. Some T. A.s teach a class. Other T. A.s help professors. At some schools, freshman classes are very large—100 to 300 students. In these classes, the professor gives lectures. Then the T. A. meets with smaller groups of students (usually on a different day) in **discussion sections.** In discussion sections, students can ask the T. A. questions and talk about homework. Like professors, some T. A.s also have **office hours**—a time when students can come to their office and ask questions.

Most students worry about their **GPA**—grade point average. In each class, they usually receive a **grade**. The GPA is the average of all of a student's grades in all his or her classes. The system works like this:

Grades	Meanings
A = 4.0	excellent
B = 3.0	very good
C = 2.0	average; OK
D = 1.0	poor
F = 0.1	failing

Practice. Compare the system above to the college/university system in your country (or a country that you know about). Discuss this with a partner.

Listening

listening Strategy

Understanding Numbers Audio

Numbers that end in *-teen* can sound similar to numbers that end in *-ty*. Listen to these numbers and pay attention to

* the stress (the accent)
* the pronunciation of the *t*

13	30	17	70
14	40	18	80
15	50	19	90
16	60		

As you hear, in numbers that end in *-teen*, the *t* really sounds like a *t*. For numbers that end in *-ty*, the *t* sounds more like a *d*.

A. Listening to Numbers. `Audio`   Listen to the numbers. Circle the one that you hear in each pair.

1. 13   30   **6.** 18   80   **11.** 16   60

2. 14   40   **7.** 19   90   **12.** 17   70

3. 15   50   **8.** 13   30   **13.** 18   80

4. 16   60   **9.** 14   40   **14.** 19   90

5. 17   70   **10.** 15   50

B. Numbers in Sentences. `Audio`   Fill in the blanks with the numbers that you hear.

1. Almost _____ percent of the class can speak another language.

2. He started college when he was _____.

3. Roughly _____ percent of all high school graduates went to college.

4. They moved to Kenya when she was _____.

5. The average age is _____.

6. Many students lived in dormitories _____ years ago.

7. She graduated _____ years ago.

8. He got married when he was _____.

9. She moved into a dormitory when she was _____.

10. A person who is _____ or _____ can enjoy college more than someone who is

_____ or _____.

C. Listening for the Main Idea: Part One. `Audio`   Listen to the first part of the radio program. Listen for the answer to this question and circle the letter of the answer.

• How different is college these days (in the United States) from college fifty years ago?

   a. Very different

   b. A little different

listening Strategy

Listening for Details **Audio**

Details are small points. They aren't as general as the main idea, but they are important because they **support** ("hold up" or explain) the main idea. Details are often examples or numbers.

D. Listening for Details. **Audio**   Now listen again to Arthur Levine's answer. As you listen, fill in this chart. If necessary, listen several times.

	50 Years Ago	Today
High school graduates going to college	15%	
Men/women		
Average age		
Ethnicity (group of people)		
Full-time/part-time		

E. Listening for the Main Idea: Part Two. **Audio**   Listen to another part of the radio program. Listen for the answer to this question and circle the letter of the answer.

- *In general,* what advice do you hear?

    a. Try everything and enjoy college.

    b. Study extra hard and try to graduate early.

F. Listening for Details. **Audio**   Now listen again to the second part. Fill in the blanks as you listen. Use the words in the box. If necessary, listen several times.

Words					Numbers
appeals	history	laundry	professors	strangers	30 40
college	joy	out	reading	younger	

Oh, I would—I—I'd have a couple of piece of—pieces of advice. I'd say, take enough quarters for

_____laundry_____. Talk to _____ because this is the big chance to meet people very unlike
    1   **2**

you. I would say talk to _____, go to office hours. If you find a class that _____
                   3   **4**

to you, even ask them for extra _____. They'll—they'll kiss your feet in amazement and
                           5

_____. I would say try everything, you know—Thai dance, botany, South American
    6

_____—because no one cares if you turn out to be not any good at it. You know, you're in
    7

_____, and you're supposed to be experimenting. And my last piece of advice to a student
    8

on the _____ end of the range, the 17- or 18-year-old, would be: think about dropping
       9

_____ because very often those years of 18, 19, and 20, campuses are forced to do a lot more
   10

babysitting than they probably should. It's people who are 20, _____, _____
                                       11   **12**

that really enjoy and get a great deal out of the undergraduate investment.

G. Listening for the Main Idea: Part Three. `Audio` Now listen to the last part of the program.
As you listen, try to answer this question:

* Who is Jeff (the caller)?

H. Listening for Details. `Audio` Read these questions. Then listen again to Jeff's advice. Write
the answers.

1. Who should the students seek out?

_____

2. Who should students talk to?

_____

3. What shouldn't students worry about?

_____

4. What should students do for the first couple of years?

_____

_____

After Listening

A. Discussion. **Group**   Discuss the answers to these questions. Then report one of your group's answers to the class.

1. Look at your chart on page 40. How are American colleges today different from colleges in your country? (If you aren't sure, say what you *think*.)

2. Did any advice on the radio show surprise you? If so, what?

3. Is any advice on the radio show different from advice in your culture? If so, what?

B. Finding Meaning behind the Words.   Anne Matthews gave this advice in the radio interview. What did she mean? Choose the best meaning for each quotation. Then compare your answers with a partner's.

1. "Take enough quarters for laundry." =

   a. Always have money.

   b. Carry only coins, not paper money, because it's dangerous to carry a lot of money.

   c. If you live on campus, you'll have to wash your own clothes. Be prepared for coin washing machines.

2. "I would say talk to professors, go to office hours. If you find a class that appeals to you, even ask them for extra reading. They'll kiss your feet in amazement and joy." =

   a. Americans kiss people's feet when they are happy.

   b. Professors kiss the feet of their best students.

   c. Professors are very happy when students want extra reading. Nobody really kisses feet.

C. Taking a Survey.   Talk to three to four people. These can be friends, classmates, teachers, neighbors, or workers at your school. Ask each person this question and fill in the chart.

• What advice can you give to students who are just beginning college?

Person	Advice

D. Discussing Survey Results. `Class` Tell the class about your survey. Did any advice surprise you? Was any advice similar to advice in Part Two or Part Four?

.::::: Part Five Academic English: Keys to Academic Success

Before Listening

A. Predicting. `Pair` In Parts Two and Four, you heard advice for students beginning college. In Part Five, you'll hear a lecture to ESL students by a college counselor. What will he say? Will his advice be different from the other advice? Make predictions. Make a list.

_____

_____

_____

_____

B. Vocabulary Preparation. The lecture has some words that may be new to you. Here are some of them. They are underlined. Guess their meanings from the context. Circle the letter of each answer.

1. The <u>key</u> to success is education. Without a good education, it's very difficult to be successful.

    a. something that goes in a door

    b. something that helps you to reach a goal

    c. something that makes a person rich

2. The <u>process</u> of choosing a good college isn't fast or easy. You probably need about a year. In this process, you need to (1) get catalogs from different schools, (2) read them, (3) visit campuses, and (4) talk with many people.

    a. choice of a school

    b. need

    c. steps

3. I want to choose my major carefully. It's important for my future <u>career</u>.

    a. studies

    b. most important area of study; major

    c. profession; work

4. First, you need to <u>set</u> your goals. Then you need a plan: How are you going to reach your goal?

    a. decide on

    b. reach

    c. put

 listening Strategy

Taking Lecture Notes

When you take lecture notes, you should put them in good order, if possible. There are many ways to do this. Here are two.

1. Put **general** ("larger") ideas or points to the left. Indent and put **specific** ("smaller") points to the right.

    Example:

Social Sciences
      Psychology
      Sociology
      Anthropology
            Cultural Anthropology
            Physical Anthropology
      Political Science
Natural Sciences
      Biology
            Microbiology
            Molecular Biology
      Chemistry
      Physics

2. Write lecture notes in a formal **outline.**

    Example:

   I. Social Sciences
     A. Psychology

B. Sociology

C. Anthropology

   1. Cultural Anthropology

   2. Physical Anthropology

D. Political Science

II. Natural Sciences

  A. Biology

    1. Microbiology

    2. Molecular Biology

  B. Chemistry

  C. Physics

Sometimes your professor will give you part of an outline. You will fill in the rest of it during the lecture.

C. Organizing General and Specific Points. Pair   Here is a list of some libraries, services, and activities for students at one U.S. university. Use the list and follow these steps.

1. There is no order to the list. Which items are more general? Write *gen* next to these items.

2. Write *L* next to libraries, *S* next to services, and *A* next to activities.

3. Put the items in order on the outline on page 46.

Tennis	Art Library
Services	Football
Chess Club	Medical Library
Research Library	Mathematics Lab
Student Health Clinic	Basketball
Labs	Karate Club
Career Planning Office	Swimming
International Student Club	Writing Lab
Clubs	University Library System
Undergraduate Library	Activities
Soccer	Lecture Note Service
Language Lab	Sports
Engineering Library	ATMs
Ski Club	Child Care Center

Outline

I. University Library System

    A.

    B.

    C.

    D.

    E.

II. Services

    A.

    B.

    C.

        1. Language Lab

        2.

        3.

    D.

    E.

    F.

III. Activities

    A.

        1. Tennis

        2.

        3.

        4.

        5.

    B.

        1. Chess Club

        2.

        3.

        4.

Listening

listening Strategy

Understanding New Words (Audio)

Professors often give definitions of new words in their lectures. Sometimes a definition is immediately after a new word.

Examples: A **goal** is <u>a carefully planned purpose</u>.

You need to highlight important points with a **felt-tip pen**—<u>a thick yellow, orange, or green pen</u>.

Also, listen for these clues:

• I mean . . . /This means . . .

• This is . . .

• In other words, . . .

A. Listening for the Meaning of a New Word. (Audio) Listen to these words in sentences from the lecture. You'll hear the sentences two times. Write the definitions that you hear.

1. academic = _____

_____

2. self-assessment = _____

_____

3. skills = _____

_____

4. values = _____

_____

5. transition = _____

_____

academic Strategy

Organizing Your Notes (Audio)

Professors often use special words in lectures. The words help you to organize your notes. Listen for words such as these: *first, second, third* (etc.), *next, one, another, then, finally,* and *last.*

When you hear these words, move down to the next line in your notes or on your outline.

Practice. Listen to one part of the lecture—Part IV on the outline (Developing Academic Skills), on page 49. Fill in *just this part* of the outline. Listen for the special words in the list above. The words will tell you when to move to a new line. If necessary, listen several times.

B. Taking Notes: Using an Outline. (Audio) Listen to the lecture and fill in as much of the outline as you can. Start at the beginning. Don't worry if you can't fill in much. (You'll listen to the lecture again in Exercise C.)

Keys to Academic Success

Introduction

I. Self-assessment = _____

   A. You can understand your—

      1. _____

      2. _____

      3. _____

      4. _____

   B. Places to take a self-assessment test

      1. _____

      2. _____

      3. _____

II. Setting a Goal

   A. Goals for different time periods

   B. Plan of action for your goal

III. Knowing the College Culture and Environment

    A. How to learn about this

        1. Study _____

        2. Find out _____

        3. Study _____

        4. Read _____

        5. _____

    B. Important because

        1. _____

        2. _____

IV. Developing Academic Skills

    A. _____

    B. _____

    C. _____

    D. _____

    E. _____

    F. _____

V. Transition to the World of Work

    A. Part-time job

    B. _____

        1. _____

        2. Write a résumé

        3. _____

        4. Find _____

C. Finding Important Information. `Audio`   Listen again to the lecture. Fill in more of the outline. As you listen, try to answer this question:

• There are five keys to academic success. Which one is most important, in the speaker's opinion?

To answer this question, pay attention when the speaker

✓ tells you that it's important

✓ emphasizes it

✓ says something more than one time

Put a star (*) next to this part of the outline.

After Listening

A. Using Your Notes. `Pair`   Use your notes to discuss these questions about the lecture.

1. What is important to know about yourself?

2. Where can you take a self-assessment test?

3. How can you learn about your college?

4. In the speaker's opinion, what's probably the most important key to academic success? Why do you think so?

B. Getting to Know College Campuses. (Pair) Here is a list of 15 places at Valley College. After this is a list of things that you might need to do. Where can you go for each one? Put letters in the blanks. Use a dictionary if necessary.

_____ **1.** Admissions Office   _____ **9.** Lecture Note Service

_____ **2.** Campus Security Escort Service   _____ **10.** Research Library

_____ **3.** Career Planning Office   _____ **11.** Snack Shack

_____ **4.** Child Care Center   _____ **12.** Travel Service

_____ **5.** College Dental Clinic   _____ **13.** Valley Ticket Service

_____ **6.** Copy Center   _____ **14.** Writing Tutorial Lab

_____ **7.** Crisis Helpline   _____ **15.** XKVC Campus Radio

_____ **8.** Recreation Center

_a._ You need to go to a dentist, but you don't have a lot of money.

_b._ A musical group from your country is going to give a concert downtown. You want to get tickets.

_c._ You were absent yesterday. You need to copy your friend's lecture notes. You want to make a photocopy.

_d._ You're very, very unhappy. You can't sleep at night. You worry all the time.

_e._ You want to buy the lecture notes for one of your classes. You want to compare them to your own notes.

_f._ You want an inexpensive plane ticket to your country for summer vacation.

_g._ You want to take a class, but you have a small child. You don't have a babysitter.

_h._ You are wondering (asking yourself this): What are possible jobs for people with my major?

_i._ Your friend wants to come to Valley College. Your friend needs an application form.

_j._ You want lunch.

_k._ You need to find an article from _Business Week_ magazine from last year.

_l._ It's difficult for you to write compositions in English. You need help.

_m._ You're at the library very late at night. You have to walk to the bus stop. You're nervous because you think that it's dangerous.

_n._ You just finished a difficult week. You need to relax by a pool.

_o._ You think, "It would be fun to work for a radio station."

Step Beyond

You're going to find out about one college library, service, or activity.

A. Doing Research

Step One

To begin, choose *one* of the following:

• The college that you go to now

• The college that you want to go to

• Any college near your home

• The school that you go to now

Step Two

Get a copy of the **catalog** for the college that you chose. (A catalog is a book with a lot of important information about a college or university. You can get one from the college or from a public library.) (Note: For a school with no catalog, ask your teacher for a list of offices, services, and activities at your school.)

Look near the front of this catalog. There will be pages with lists of the college's libraries, services, and activities.

Find one interesting library, service, or activity. Read about it in the catalog.

B. Brainstorming. Group   Tell your group about your choice. What did you learn about it from the catalog? What more do you want to know? Write four to five questions.

speaking Strategy

Interviewing

Sometimes you'll need to interview people. In an interview, you generally ask a person a number of questions about one topic. (In a survey, you generally ask many people the same question.)

To begin an interview, you can say the following:

• Excuse me. Could I ask you a few questions for a class?

• Hi. I'm doing a project for my English class. May I ask you a few questions?

• Hello. My name's _____. May I ask you a few short questions for a project in my English class?

During the interview, do the following:

- Listen to the answers.
- Show interest. (Say "Oh?" "Really?" "That's interesting.")
- Take notes. (Remember to bring a pen and paper.)
- Don't be shy. If you don't understand something, ask the person to repeat.

To end the interview, you can say the following:

- Well, thanks a lot.
- Thank you for your time.
- Thanks for your help.

C. Interviewing.
For homework, interview one person. This person should know about the library, service, or activity that you chose. (For example, go to a counselor in the Career Planning Office or a security guard at Campus Security.) Ask this person your questions from Exercise B, Brainstorming.

D. Reporting Interview Results. Class
What did you learn about the college? Tell the class one interesting thing that you learned from your interview.

From Part One, page 22: D. Ranking Values

Americans:
  #1: children's education
  #8: work

Europeans:
  #1: children's education
  #4: work

Japanese:
  #1: health
  #2: work

Source: International Research Associates and the Roper Organization, reported in *American Demographics*, May 1989, v. 11 n. 5, p. 19.

chapter Two

Free Enterprise

In this chapter, you'll listen to information about and discuss selling products internationally.

Part One Introduction: Advertising Messages

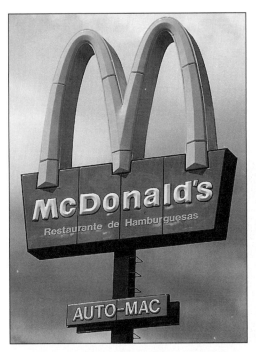

A few products with international markets

A. *Thinking Ahead.* Pair   You are going to look at and discuss a magazine **advertisement** (or **ad**). Before you look at it, do these activities.

1. Describe an ad that you like. It can be from a magazine, TV, radio or any other place. Say why you like it.

   Example: I like the new Macintosh computer ads because they are funny.

2. Describe an ad that you *don't* like. Say why you don't like it.

   Example: I don't like the new ads for the soft drink because they are in black and white, and not in color.

3. Describe a clothing ad or a perfume ad from your country.

B. *Reading an Ad.*   Study this ad. Try to answer the following questions:

• What product is the company advertising?

• Where do you think the product comes from?

C. *Discussion.* Group   Discuss the answers to these questions.

1. What product is the company advertising?

2. Who is the **target audience** for the ad? In other words, who is the ad for, in your opinion? Is it for someone like you? For someone older? Someone younger? Someone in the United States? Someone in another country?

3. In your opinion, is this an **effective** ad? In other words, does it make you want to buy the product?

4. Would this ad be effective in any country in the world? Why or why not?

D. Journal Writing.   Choose *one* of these topics. Write about it for five minutes. Don't worry about grammar and don't use a dictionary. Just put as many ideas as you can on paper.

• Describe an ad that you like. What is the product? Who is the target audience?

• Describe an ad that you don't like. What is the product? Who is the audience?

• Describe a foreign product that you can buy where you live. Where is it from? Why do people want to buy it? What kind of advertising does it have?

....::::: Part Two Everyday English:
                           The Advertising Age

Before Listening

 *listening* **Strategy**

Brainstorming

Sometimes you know the topic of something that you are going to listen to. When this happens, it's a good idea to brainstorm. Brainstorming is thinking of ideas that you have on a topic *before* you listen. You can brainstorm alone or in a group. When you brainstorm, you can talk about your ideas, write them down, or just think about them. This prepares you for listening. Also, it helps you to understand what you are going to hear.

A. Brainstorming: Making a List.   In this part, you are going to listen to students talking about products. The products come from other countries, but people buy them in the United States. Fill in the chart. Follow these directions.

1. Make a list of products that you use often. You can include clothing items.

2. Where was each item made? Look for the country. (Hint: Look for labels or writing on the objects themselves. Look for "Made in _____" or "Imported from _____.") Write the information in the chart.

Object	Where It Is Made
pen	Japan

B. Discussion. **Pair**   Talk about the objects in your chart. Answer these questions.

1. Compare the objects in your chart with those in your partner's chart. Are any objects the same? What are they? Are any countries the same? What are they?

2. Describe each object from another country. Is it good quality?

3. Is the item expensive or inexpensive?

4. Where did you buy this object? Where can people buy objects like it?

5. Have you ever seen an ad for the object? If so, describe it. Is it an effective ad? Why or why not?

C. Vocabulary Preparation.

C. Vocabulary Preparation.   In the conversation in this part, the students will use some common informal words. Do you know the words? First, read them in the following short conversations. They are underlined. Then, in the lists below, find the meanings of the informal words. Write the letters in the blanks.

Conversations

1. A: Do you like that Levi's ad?

    B: <u>Nope</u>. I hate it.

2. A: Do you like the Gap ad?

    B: <u>Yeah</u>, it's nice.

3. A: What's all that <u>stuff</u> in your backpack?

    B: That's my lunch, my English book, my glasses, my new pen . . .

4. A: Do you think my new hat looks good on me?

    B: Yes, in fact, it looks very <u>cool</u>!

5. A: How much did your new hat cost?

    B: Five <u>bucks</u>.

6. A: How do you like my new shirt?

    B: Wow! It's <u>wild</u>. The colors are so bright, they hurt my eyes!

7. A: So, the next day, I called Drew, and he said . . .

    B: <u>Whoa</u>, it's later than I thought! We have to get going now!

Informal Words

_g_	**1.** nope	
_____	**2.** yeah	
_____	**3.** stuff	
_____	**4.** cool	
_____	**5.** bucks	
_____	**6.** wild	
_____	**7.** whoa	

Meanings

a. things, objects, or activities

b. extreme, unusual, or intense

c. dollars

d. Wait a minute . . .

e. nice

f. yes

g. no

Listening

A. Listening for Main Ideas. **Video/Audio**   Listen to the conversation. Brandon and Chrissy talk about new products that they've bought recently. The products are from **overseas** (other countries). As you listen, try to answer these questions:

- What products did the students buy?
- Why did they buy them?

B. Listening for Details. **Video/Audio**   Now listen again. As you listen, complete the chart.

Objects	Country They Are From
	China
Chrissy's shoes	
	England

C. Listening for Descriptive Language. (Video/Audio) Listen again. This time, you are going to hear only part of the conversation. As you listen, listen for the descriptive words (adjectives) in the box. Write them in the blanks.

Descriptive Words

American	curious	odd
bad	little	old
British	local (use it two times)	wild (use it two times)

Note: Use a dictionary to find the meanings of any words that are new to you.

Brandon: Hey, speaking of stuff made overseas, have you seen that new ad for SuperMints?

Chrissy: I don't know . . .

Brandon: It's really ____wild____. There are all these _____ couples—an
                         1   **2**

      _____ lady and a _____ boy, a woman and her dog, two
                         3   **4**

      guys—and one wants to kiss the other.

Chrissy: Oh, yeah, but the other refuses because the one that wants a kiss has

      _____ breath!
                         5

Brandon: Yeah, it's done in _____ colors and settings, like a music video. I was
                              6

      so _____, I bought some. I noticed they're from England and I was
                 7

      wondering if the commercial is _____, too. It just didn't look
                                      8

      _____.
                 9

Chrissy: I don't know. I think they remake commercials for the country they want to sell

      the product in because you have to appeal to the _____ market. You've
                                                              10

      got to relate the product to _____ values.
                                   11

Brandon: Yeah. And there's stuff you can do in commercials in other countries that you *sure*

      can't do here.

listening Strategy

Listening for Supporting Information (Audio)

When people give ideas or opinions, they often give support for the ideas. Sometimes you hear the word *because*—this tells you supporting information is following. Other times, an example or an explanation follows without the word *because*.

Examples: I don't buy clothes that are made overseas ***because*** *I want to support American workers.*

Your new shoes are really wild; *the high heels and that bright green color are very fashionable!*

D. Listening for Supporting Information. (Video/Audio) Listen to the same part of the conversation again. This time listen for the information that supports or explains the statements. Write the information.

1. That SuperMints commercial is really wild.

Supporting information: _____

_____

2. I think they remake commercials for the country they want to sell the product in.

Supporting information: _____

_____

After Listening

A. Information Gap. (Pair) Work with a partner. One of you works on page 64. The other works on page 219. Don't look at your partner's page. Take turns asking and answering questions about imported food products in a catalog. Write the answers in the blanks on your catalog page.

Ask the following:

- Where is the product from?

- How much does it weigh? Or: How much is there?

- How much does it cost? Or: How much do they cost?

Student A

Ask questions to complete this catalog page. Then answer your partner's questions.

Gourmet Gulch . . . *bringing you the finest in imported food products.*

Parma Ham
Imported from _____
Weight: 20 lbs.
$ _____

Smoked Salmon
Flown in daily from Scotland
Weight: _____
$35.00

Fancy Arare Crackers
Made in Japan
Weight: 1 lb.
$ _____

Coffee Beans
Imported from _____
Includes: _____
$50.00

Note: The abbreviation lb. = pound; the abbreviation lbs. = pounds.

B. Taking a Survey.   Talk to three classmates. Ask their opinion about foreign-made products. Write their answers in the chart.

Example: A: What foreign-made products do you buy?

B: I buy foreign-made clothing and cosmetics.

A: Why do you buy them?

B: The clothing is cheap, and the cosmetics are good quality.

Student	Student 1	Student 2	Student 3
Name	_____	_____	_____
Country	_____	_____	_____
Part 1			
1. What foreign-made products do you buy? *Examples:* food, clothing, electronics.			
2. Why do you buy them?			
3. How do they compare with the same items from another country?			
Part 2			
1. Have you ever eaten at a U.S. restaurant chain *inside* the United States?	☐ Yes ☐ No	☐ Yes ☐ No	☐ Yes ☐ No
2. Have you ever eaten at a U.S. restaurant chain *outside* the United States?	☐ Yes ☐ No	☐ Yes ☐ No	☐ Yes ☐ No
3. If your answers to questions 1 and 2 are yes, how did the food and service compare in the two locations?			
Part 3			
Write one question of your own about foreign-made products. _____ _____ _____			

C. Discussing Survey Results. (Group)   Form groups of five. Try not to be in a group with someone that you interviewed. Discuss the results of your survey. Try to answer these questions:

1. What types of foreign items do people in class buy a lot of?

2. Why do they buy these items?

3. How are fast-food restaurants alike in the United States and other countries? How are they
   different?

. . : : ┊ ┊ ┊ Part Three The Mechanics of Listening
and Speaking

Language Functions

Starting a Conversation (Audio)

There are several ways to start an informal conversation with someone you already know. Here are
some examples:

- Hi. How are you?
- Hi. What's up?
- Hi. How's it going?
- Hi. What's new?
- Hi. What have you been up to* lately?
- Hello. How have you been?

* up to = doing

Continuing a Conversation (Audio)

There are many possible answers when a friend starts a conversation. Sometimes friends give "real"
information. In other words, they say what they have been doing or how they are feeling. Other times
they give polite answers. These answers don't really give any new information. People use them all
the time, but they don't really mean very much. Here are some examples:

- Oh, nothing much. (Polite answer)
- Well, I was away last week. I went to the mountains. (Real answer)

A. Practice. [Audio] Listen to each conversation. Fill in the blanks with the words that you hear.

1. A: Hi. _____What's up?_____

   B: Oh, nothing much.

2. A: Hi. How's it going?

   B: Great! How's it going _____?

3. A: Hi. _____?

   B: Hi! I just got a new cat. That's what's new!

4. A: Hi. What have you _____ lately?

   B: I've been really busy studying for the TOEFL exam.

5. A: Hi. How are you?

   B: Hi! Just great. _____?

B. Practice. [Pair] One of you plays the role of Student A, and the other is Student B. Follow the directions in the boxes. Exchange roles after you do the exercise three times.

Example: A: Hi! How's it going?

   B: I'm tired! I stayed up all night studying!

Student A

You haven't seen your friend for a week. Say hello and greet him or her with a conversation starter. (See page 66.)

Student B

You meet a friend. Your friend starts a conversation. Continue the conversation. Choose one of the options.

Option 1:   You stayed up all night studying for an exam. You're tired.

Option 2:   What a day! You've just won $1,000 in the lottery.

Option 3:   You are having a terrible week. Yesterday you were in a car accident. Today you lost your job. Also, you have a cold.

Option 4:   You're late for class, but you're happy to see your friend.

Option 5:   You have a very boring life. Nothing exciting has happened to you in a long time.

Option 6:   You have a very exciting life. You saved a child who fell into a fountain. A TV news crew came and interviewed you. You were on the news last night!

Pronunciation

Reduced Forms of Words (Audio)

When people speak quickly, some words become reduced, or short. Here are some examples.

Long Form	Short From
What's up?	Whasup?
How is it going?	Howzit going?
What have you been up to?	Whatuv you been up to?
How *about you*?	How 'boutchu?
How *are you doing*?	How ya doin?
I don't have a *lot of* money.	I don't have a lotta money.
I *don't know.*	I dunno.

C. Practice. (Audio)   Listen to this conversation. You'll hear the reductions. Write the long form of the words in the blanks.

A: Hi. _____What's up_____?
                        1

B: Hi. Not much. _____ going with you?
                              2

A: I _____. I've been pretty busy lately. _____ you been up to?
                3   **4**

B: I've been pretty busy, too. _____ doing in English?
                                          5

A: Not bad, but it's a _____ work.
                              6

Intonation

Wh- Questions **Audio**

When you ask a question with a *wh-* word (*who, what, when, where, why,* and *how*), your voice goes down at the end of the sentence. Here are some examples:

- What's up?

- How's it going?

- What have you been doing lately?

- What's new with you?

- How are you?

D. Practice. **Audio**   Compare a *wh-* question with a *yes-no* question. Read these examples as you listen to the tape. Then answer this question: *How is the intonation in these two questions different?*

1. How are you?

2. Are you OK?

E. Practice. **Audio**   Listen to the following questions. If you hear a *wh-* question, circle the down arrow (↘). If you hear a *yes-no* question, circle the up arrow (↗).

F. Practice. (Pair) Ask and answer six questions about what you are wearing. Ask both *wh-* questions and *yes-no* questions. Make sure your intonation goes up for the *yes-no* questions, and down for the *wh-* questions. Listen to each other's intonation. Help your partner if he or she makes a mistake.

Examples: A: Where did you get those shoes?

B: I bought them at a shoe store downtown.

A: Do you like my new shirt?

B: Yeah. It's really wild.

Review: Language Functions

Starting a Conversation (Video/Audio)

Listen to these examples of how to start a conversation. They'll help you to do the next section.

Put It Together

A. Starting Conversations. Group You are going to start conversations with your classmates.

Step One

Make a list of your recent activities. Write down things that you have done this week.

Recent Activities

Step Two

Divide the class into two teams, Team A and Team B.

- Members of Team A will start conversations with as many members of Team B as possible in five minutes. They will write down how many people with whom they started a conversation within the time limit. They will use the expressions in the list in the box.

- Members of Team B will use their Recent Activities lists to continue the conversation, or they will just give polite answers. They will use the expressions in the box below.

Then teams change roles. The team that started the most conversations wins.

Conversation Starters and Answers

A: Hi. What's up?
B: Oh, nothing much.

A: Hi. How's it going?
B: Great! How's it going with you?

A: Hi! What's new?
B: Not much. What's new with you?

A: Hi. How are you?
B: Hi! Just great. How are you?

A: Hi. What have you been up to lately?
B: Oh, you know . . . (fill in with recent activities)

B. Talking about the Week. (Pair) Each student has a blank one-week agenda. This is a calendar.
You write your daily activities on it.

Write all your activities for the past week on the agenda.

S	M	T	W	T	F	S
			1	2	3	4	5
6	7	8	9	10	11	12
13	14	15	16	17	18	19
20	21	22	23	24	25	26
27	28	29	30			

Week of _____ to _____

MONDAY

TUESDAY

WEDNESDAY

THURSDAY

FRIDAY

SATURDAY

SUNDAY

Step Two

- Take turns starting a conversation with your partner. Use the conversation starters on page 66.

- Answer with real information. Look at your agenda for information.

- Ask one or two questions to continue the conversation. Remember to use correct question intonation.

  Example: A: Hi. What have you been up to lately?

  B: Well, yesterday I played soccer.

  A: Really? Do you play a lot of soccer?

  B: Yeah. I usually play on Sunday in the park with friends. And this week we played on Saturday, too.

. . : : : : **Part Four** Broadcast English: Mista Donatsu

Before Listening

 listening **Strategy**

Predicting

Sometimes you can make a prediction about a radio or TV program, or even a college lecture, just from the title or topic. In other words, you can guess the kind of information the program or lecture might contain. When you make a prediction, it prepares you for listening. Also, it helps you to understand what you are going to hear.

A. Predicting. **Group**   You are going to hear a radio interview about an American food chain, Mister Donut. It has opened donut shops in Japan. Make predictions about Mister Donut in Japan. Discuss the answers to these questions.

1. Do you think that the donut restaurants will be the same in the United States and a foreign country? Why or why not?

2. If you think the restaurants will be different, what things might be different?

3. Do you think a donut shop in Japan has the same kind of donuts as in the United States? Explain your answer.

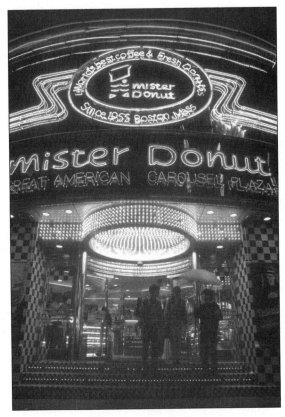

A Mister Donut shop in Japan

 listening Strategy

Guessing Meaning from Context

You can often guess the meanings of new words that you hear. Pay attention to clues in words before or after the new word.

B. Guessing Meaning from Context.   You are going to hear a radio interview. It's about a donut shop in Japan. Before you listen, guess the meanings of some words from the program. The words are underlined in the sentences. Look for clues to their meanings in the words around them.

Write your guess in the blank after each sentence. Then check your guess with your teacher or the dictionary.

1. We're going to the <u>opening</u> of that new restaurant tonight—it's a special event to celebrate the start of their business.

   Guess: _The first day of business_

2. People like the <u>gracious</u> service at the new restaurant. The waiters are very polite and formal.

   Guess: _____

3. When you cook with grease or oil, the stove, walls, and even your clothes become <u>greasy</u> and hard to clean.

   Guess: _____

4. <u>Wax paper</u> is better than plastic wrap for food because food doesn't stick to it. You can easily pull off the wax paper from food.

   Guess: _____

5. He serves the coffee so quickly that it <u>sloshes</u> out of the cup and spills on the table.

   Guess: _____

6. The tables, counters, and walls in this restaurant are <u>gleaming</u>! They must clean them very carefully.

   Guess: _____

7. A waiter in Japan might call guests "<u>honorable</u> customers." This is because the customers are important and respected.

   Guess: _____

8. This restaurant serves food on expensive <u>china</u> plates instead of cheap plastic or paper dishes.

   Guess: _____

9. Martin got a job as a <u>disk jockey</u> at a radio station in Japan. Listeners can't understand what he is saying, but they like the way that he announces the music.

   Guess: _____

10. Martin plays only <u>goldie oldies</u>—rock 'n' roll music from the 50s and 60s.

    Guess: _____

11. I really like this restaurant because coffee <u>refills</u> don't cost extra.

Guess: _____

12. You can make <u>caramel</u> candy by cooking sugar at a high temperature.

Guess: _____

13. This drink is a strange <u>concoction</u>—it's a mixture of orange juice and carrot juice.

Guess: _____

C. Idioms, Slang, and Phrasal Verbs.   Here are some examples of idioms, slang, and phrasal verbs that you will hear in the radio interview. Each one has a meaning in the list on the right. Write the letter of the meaning next to the expression that it matches.

Idioms, Slang, or Phrasal Verbs   **Meanings**

____*d*____ **1.** to take by storm   *a.* to claim or say something

_____ **2.** dirt cheap   *b.* to get the better result in an exchange

_____ **3.** to purport to be   *c.* to discuss

_____ **4.** to pour out of   *d.* to be very popular

_____ **5.** to talk over   *e.* to exit a place quickly, with a lot of other people

_____ **6.** to get the better end   *f.* very inexpensive
           of a bargain

D. Understanding Words with Several Meanings.   Many words in English have more than one meaning. The word *draw* means "make pictures with a pen or pencil." Here are two other meanings of *draw*. They are both nouns. Match each meaning to the context. Write the letters in the blanks.

a. something that people like and that they go in large numbers to get

b. not a win or a loss

_____ **1.** Many people go to that restaurant. What's the <u>draw</u>? Can you tell me the reason for its success?

_____ **2.** I like the donuts at this store. But I like the service at that store. I can't decide which I like better. It's a <u>draw</u>.

Listening

A. Listening for the Main Idea. (Audio)   Listen to the radio interview. As you listen, try to answer this question:

• Is Mister Donut successful in Japan?

B. Listening for Supporting Information. (Audio)   Now listen again. As you listen, find reasons that support your answer to the question in Exercise A, Is Mister Donut successful in Japan? List the reasons here:

Reasons

_____

_____

_____

_____

_____

C. Listening for Details. (Audio)   Listen again to part of the interview. According to T. R. Reid, Mister Donut does something wrong. What is it?

_____

_____

D. Listening for Comparisons. (Audio)   How does Mister Donut in Japan compare with Mister Donut in the United States? Listen again for these points of comparison and fill in the chart.

	Mister Donut in Japan	Mister Donut in the U.S.
Restaurant Appearance		
Waiters' Uniforms	perfect, white cap, bow tie	greasy apron
Service		
Food		

E. Japanese Words and Phrases. (Audio)   T. R. Reid uses some Japanese words and Japanese-sounding words in the interview. He tells you what they mean. Listen again for these words and their meanings. Then write the meanings in the blanks next to the Japanese (Japanese-sounding words).

Example: "They're there because it's *kakoi*—it's cool."

        Meaning: *Kakoi* means "cool."

Japanese (Japanese-Sounding) Words	Meanings
1. *Mista Donatsu*	_____
2. *lucky caado*	_____
3. *koati*	_____

After Listening

A. Discussion. (Group)   Discuss the answers to these questions.

1. Would Mister Donut be successful in other countries? Explain your answer.

2. What American fast-food restaurants are popular outside the United States? Why do you think they are popular?

3. What are your favorite fast-food restaurants? How are they like the restaurants in the radio interview? How are they different?

B. Brainstorming: Designing a Restaurant. (Pair)   Think of a fast-food restaurant to open near your school. You want your restaurant to draw students. Complete the chart. Share your descriptions with the class. Then the class votes on the best restaurant.

Kind of food	
Place (music, dishes, decoration)	
Any special draw (such as coffee refills)	

.:::: **Part Five** Academic English: Selling Snapple in Japan

Before Listening

A. Brainstorming. **Group**   You are going to listen to a lecture about a U.S. **beverage** (drink) company. Before you listen, brainstorm for ideas about cold beverages. Think about drink types, ingredients, and words that describe the drinks. (For example: How do cold beverages make you feel? How do they taste? Why do you drink them?) You'll see a few examples in the box below.

Types	Ingredients	Descriptions
soda	fruit	sweet
iced tea	tea	bitter
orange juice	fruit	sweet, refreshing, healthful

B. Guessing Meaning from Context.   You are going to hear a lecture about selling a U.S. beverage in Japan. You are going to hear a lot of words that describe drinks. Before you listen, guess the meanings of some words from the lecture. The words are underlined in the sentences. Look for clues to their meanings in the words around them.

Write your guess in the blank after each sentence. Then check your guess with your teacher or the dictionary.

1. Many Americans like juice drinks that have <u>fruit pulp</u>—little pieces of fruit—floating in them.

   Guess: _Little pieces of fruit_ _____

2. I found an orange <u>seed</u> in my juice—I think I'll plant it and see if it will grow into a tree.

   Guess: _____

3. Juice is very <u>thirst-quenching</u>. However, soda always leaves me thirsty.

   Guess: _____

4. Juice is a wholesome and <u>nutritious</u> drink because it contains vitamins. It's good for your health.

   Guess: _____

5. This drink is very popular because it is made from natural ingredients, a <u>highly desirable trait</u>.

   Guess: _____

C. Vocabulary: The Word Market.   You are going to hear many words and expressions for marketing. **Marketing** means getting products from the manufacturer to the customer. First, study these forms of the word *market*. Then fill in the blanks in the passage that follows with the correct form of the word *market*. Use each form once.

Nouns

- a **market** or a **marketplace:** customers; a place, country, region, or group of people that buys a product

- a **marketer:** a person who works to sell a product

- **marketing:** the act of getting a product from manufacturer to customer

Verb

- to **market:** to get a product from manufacturer to customer

---

Marketing Overseas

A company with a successful product wants to sell its product overseas. The first step in this process is to gather information about the foreign _____*market*_____. The company finds the answer to this
                                                                                                 1

question: Will the product be popular in the new _____? Good _____ learn about
                                                                          2   3

the culture of the new country. They do research. Sometimes a company decides to change a product

for a different country. Sometimes it may decide not to _____ the product at all in the other
                                                                                   4

country. When a company does decide to sell a product in a new country, it must also find out the best

way to advertise the product. Research also helps the company to design an effective marketing cam-

paign. Because of all this, the _____ of a product in a new country is a complex process:
                                                              5

This is true even for a product successful in another country.

D. Vocabulary: Marketing and Selling.

There are many other words and expressions in the lecture for marketing and selling. Try to guess their meanings. Look for the clues in words around them.

Write your guess in the blank after each sentence. Then check your guess with your teacher or the dictionary.

1. The purpose of advertising is <u>to generate a positive attitude toward</u> a product so people will like it and want to buy it.

   Guess: _To make people like something_____

2. Levi's jeans are popular in many <u>segments</u> of the clothing market; for example, teen-aged boys, teen-aged girls, middle-aged men, and middle-aged women.

   Guess: _____

3. Quaker Oats is a <u>consumer goods</u> company. It makes products that people buy and use quickly such as food and beverages.

   Guess: _____

4. The displays in the store had a lot of <u>customer traffic</u>: lots of people came up to look at them all day long.

   Guess: _____

5. Unfortunately, there wasn't much <u>demand</u> for that product. Nobody wanted to buy it.

   Guess: _____

6. One way to advertise something is by <u>point-of purchase displays</u>—advertisements that appear right in the store.

   Guess: _____

7. The product had an <u>image problem</u>. It didn't *look* like a good product, so people didn't buy it.

   Guess: _____

Listening

Products on display in a Japanese supermarket

A. Listening for the Main Idea. (Audio)   Listen to the lecture. It is titled "Selling Snapple in Japan." As you listen, try to answer this question:

• Were Snapple fruit drinks popular in Japan?

B. Taking Notes. (Audio)   Listen to the lecture again. This time fill in the outline.

Selling Snapple in Japan

I. Background

    A. The Quaker Oats Company

       1. ___Everyone knows it for its high-quality products._____

       2. It recently had a problem with _____

    B. Snapple in the United States

        1. Snapple beverages included _____

          _____

        2. Drinks contained _____

II. Snapple in Japan

    A. Failure in Japan after only three years

    B. Product displays

        1. Looks: _____

        2. Customer response: _____

    C. Product image problems

        1. In drinks, Japanese like _____

        2. To the Japanese, Snapple _____

    D. Attitude of Quaker marketing department

        1. It didn't believe that _____

        2. Sales will improve when Japanese realize that pulp means high quality.

III. Quaker's Possible Marketing Mistakes

    A. Mistake 1—Market research: _____

      _____

    B. Mistake 2—Advertising: _____

      _____

    C. Mistake 3—Financial: _____

      _____

C. (Optional) Checking Your Outline. **Audio** If necessary, rewind the tape and listen again to the lecture. Check your notes.

After Listening

academic Strategy

Asking Questions

Some professors like students to ask questions while they give a lecture. Others want students to wait until the lecture is over. If you have a professor who wants you to wait, write your questions as you take notes. Write them in the margin next to the point you want to ask about. Write them in another ink color. You can ask—

- for a definition of a word you don't understand

- about something that is not clear or that you didn't understand

- for more information about something that interests you

Practice: Write three questions about the lecture on selling Snapple in Japan. Try to write one of each kind (for a definition, about something that is not clear, and to get further information). Write them on the lines:

1. _____

2. _____

3. _____

A. Using Your Notes. **Pair**   Use your notes to discuss these questions about the lecture.

1. What did people in the United States like about Snapple drinks?

2. What were the Snapple displays in Japan like?

3. What didn't the Japanese like about the Snapple drinks?

4. What did the marketing people at Quaker think when they heard about the problem in Japan?

5. What were Quaker's three possible marketing mistakes?

B. Taking a Market Survey. **Group**   Quaker Oats didn't do a market survey before it decided to sell Snapple in Japan. This was a mistake. Do a market survey in class to see which type of fruit drink most of your classmates like to buy.

Step One

1. Read the survey below. Make your choice and check your favorite.

2. Then in your group, ask each student the question in the chart.

3. Write the total number of votes for each choice in the chart.

4. What's your group's favorite choice? _____ What's your group's least favorite choice? _____

Market Survey

Which fruit drink would you prefer?

Type 1: _____

One hundred percent real fruit juice, with pulp and seeds. No added sugar or vitamins.

Group Vote Total: _____

Type 2: _____

One hundred percent real fruit juice, clear without pulp and seeds. No added sugar or vitamins.

Group Vote Total: _____

Type 3: _____

Real fruit juice mixed with carbonated (soda) water and sugar. Thirteen vitamins and minerals added.

Group Vote Total: _____

Step Two

Compare your answers with those of another group. Do both groups like and dislike the same type of fruit drink?

Step Beyond

You are going to give a presentation on selling a product in a foreign country.

A. Interviewing

Step One

Think of a product made in your country. Think about the product carefully. Answer these questions about it:

- What is the product?

- What makes it special? (Useful? Attractive? Different?)

Step Two

Interview a person who is from a different country. (If you can't find one, your teacher can bring some-one to class.) Find out all you need to know to sell the product in that person's country. Do the following.

1. First, describe the product.

2. Then ask the person these questions:

   - What do you think about the product?

   - Would you buy it as it is now?

   - What changes would make the product more attractive to you?

   - What kind of advertising works best in your country?

   - What are good ways to advertise the product in your country?

Takes notes on your interview.

speaking Strategy

Eye Contact

When you give a presentation in class, make eye contact with your audience. Look at the faces of the people you are speaking to. If you are speaking to a big group, move your eyes around the room to look at everyone. Don't keep your eyes on just one member of the audience.

B. Giving a Presentation. (Class)   Now you are ready to prepare your presentation.

Step One

Decide on an advertisement for the product. Design your ad. Draw a picture of it and/or write the "copy" (the words that appear in the ad).

Step Two

Use the following outline to prepare a presentation on your product and ad design. You will give the presentation to the class or to a small group of students. Your presentation should last no more than three minutes. Remember to use good eye contact while you give your presentation.

 speaking Strategy

Outlining

Before you give a presentation to a group, it's a good idea to make an outline of what you want to say. An outline helps you to decide what you want to say and helps you stay on your subject while you are speaking. You can use the outline while you speak, but you need to look up from it frequently.

Presentation Outline

I. Description of the product:

_____

_____

_____

II. Description of the target market (the country where the product will be marketed):

_____

III. Changes in the product (Will the product be changed for this market? Why or why not? Explain how the culture of the new market might require changing the product.):

_____

_____

_____

_____

IV. Advertising in this market (What kind of advertising works best for this kind of product in this market?):

_____

_____

V. Description of your advertisement(s):

_____

_____

_____

_____

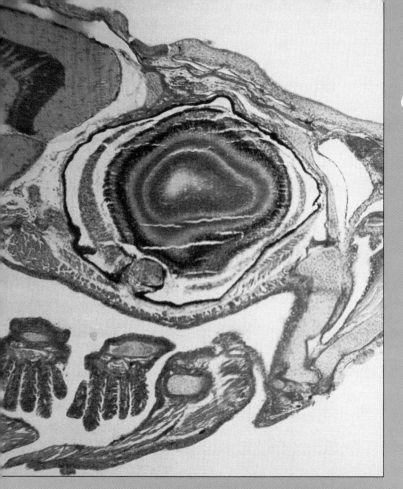

Three

Animal Behavior

In this chapter, you'll listen to and discuss information about animals' emotions and intelligence.

Part One Introduction: Animal Behavior

A. Brainstorming. **Group**   Discuss the animals in these pictures. How are they all similar? How are they different?

A human

A chimpanzee

A dolphin

A leopard

Vervet monkeys

B. Reading.   Read the three paragraphs about animal behavior. As you read, try to answer this question:

• How are some animals similar to humans?

Strange but True

Sheba is a healthy six-year-old. She is learning many things: to choose colors, to count (from zero to seven so far), to know words for body parts, and to take care of her own pet dog. Sheba is a chimpanzee.

* * * * * *

In Kenya, vervet monkeys make many different noises. Some of these noises are alarm calls—"Danger!" One call means "Snake!" When the monkeys hear this, they all look down. A different call means "Leopard!"
5 The monkeys hear this, and they run into the trees. A third call means "Eagle!" At this call, all the monkeys look up into the sky.

* * * * * *

On July 23, 1996, Martin Richardson was on a tourist boat off the coast of Egypt. A group of dolphins was jumping playfully near the boat. Richardson and two friends decided to swim with the dolphins, and they jumped into the water. Suddenly, a shark appeared and attacked Richardson. Soon the water was red
10 with his blood. Immediately, three of the dolphins swam around him. They began to hit the water again and again with their tails. They protected Richardson from the shark and saved his life.

Sources: Story of Sheba the chimpanzee, adapted from Sally Boysen, "Proving a professor's pet theory, Sheba the Chimp is treating a basset hound as her own dog" from *People Weekly* (April 18, 1988). Copyright © 1988 by Time, Inc. Reprinted with the permission of *Time*.

Story of vervet monkeys, adapted from Marian Stamp Dawkins, "The private life of the vampire bat . . . and other surprising examples of animal behavior" from *UNESCO Courier* (February 1988). Copyright © 1988 by UNESCO (France). Reprinted with the permission of the publishers.

Story of Martin Richardson and dolphins, adapted from Aline A. Newman, "Animals in action" from *Boys' Life* (March 1998) 88, no. 3. Copyright © 1998 by the Boy Scouts of America, Inc. Reprinted with the permission of *Boys' Life*.

C. Discussion. **Group**   Discuss your answers to these questions.

1. Did anything in "Strange but True" surprise you? If so, what?
2. What do the three examples in the reading show us about animals' ability to communicate, their intelligence, and their emotions?
3. Do you know any other strange-but-true animal stories? If so, tell one to your group.

D. Journal Writing.   Choose *one* of these topics. Write about it for five minutes. Don't worry about grammar and don't use a dictionary. Just put as many ideas as you can on paper.

• Write your ideas about one of the animals from "Strange but True."
• Describe an animal that a classmate told you about.
• Tell a story about any other surprising animal.

Part Two Everyday English: That Darn Cat

Before Listening

A. Brainstorming. Group   Talk about these animals. What do you know about their ability to communicate, their intelligence, and their emotions?

A domestic cat

A domestic dog

Humans

B. Taking a Survey.   Talk to your classmates, teachers, students in other classes, and workers at your school. Ask them two questions:

1. Do you have a pet? Or: Did you have a pet in the past?

2. Do animals feel emotions?

Record their answers in the box. Put a | for each answer (for example, ⫫| = 6).

Do Animals Feel Emotions?

Answers from people with pets		Answers from people without pets	
Yes	No	Yes	No

C. Discussing Survey Results. (Group) Discuss the results of the survey. Try to answer these questions:

1. Do most people with pets think that animals feel emotions?

2. Do most people without pets think that animals feel emotions?

3. Are the two groups' ideas similar?

4. Do most people think that animals feel emotions?

Listening

A. Listening for the Main Idea. (Video/Audio) Listen to the conversation. As you listen, try to answer this question:

• What do Tanya, Jennifer, and Brandon believe about animals' emotions and intelligence?

B. Listening for Reasons. (Video/Audio) Read these questions. Then listen to the conversation again. Write your answers.

1. Why does Jennifer have this cat? _____

_____

2. Why does Jennifer say, "Cats are very sensitive"? _____

_____

3. Why does Jennifer think that dolphins understand a lot? _____

_____

4. Why is Brandon sneezing? _____

_____

listening Strategy

Listening for Stressed Words (Audio)

In English, people usually stress the important words in a sentence. In other words, the important words are higher, clearer, and louder than other words.

If you understand only the stressed words in a sentence, you probably understand the important information.

Example: Is *he* going to live *here* with *us?*

C. Listening for Stressed Words. (Video/Audio)   Listen again to part of the conversation. Fill in the blanks with the stressed words. Use the words in the box.

animals	dolphins	laughs	smart
beach	don't	ocean	stupid
buy	embarrassed	push	trouble
cat	hates	save	understand
do	humans	sensitive	zillion

Jennifer: Cats are very _____*sensitive*_____. You know, sometimes when a

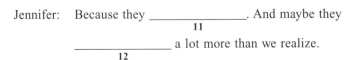

1

_____ does something kind of _____—I don't
2   3

know, falls off a table or something—and everybody _____?
4

You can just tell that the cat feels really _____. It
5

_____ to be laughed at.
6

Tanya: I _____ _____ that. Why do
7   8

people always think that _____ have the
9

same emotions that _____ have?
10

Jennifer: Because they _____. And maybe they
11

_____ a lot more than we realize.
12

Brandon: Yeah. There are a _____ stories about how
                                              13

_____ animals are.
          14

Jennifer: Like _____. You know, sometimes they
                         15

_____ a swimmer in the _____ who gets in
          16   17

_____ and can't swim back to the _____? They
          18   19

come right up, get right under the swimmer, and _____ him
                                                             20

up to the surface.

listening Strategy

Understanding Emotion from Tone of Voice Audio

It's possible to change the meaning of one word—or sentence—with a change of intonation.

Example: Yeah!   (The person agrees and is enthusiastic or excited.)

Yeah.   (The person agrees unhappily.)

Yeah . . .   (The person isn't sure and maybe even disagrees.)

The context, or situation, can also help you to understand meaning.

D. Practice. Audio   Listen to the short conversations. The second person uses the word or words
on the top line. What does this person really mean? Circle *a* or *b*.

1. okay =

a. Yes, I agree, and I'm happy about this.

b. I agree, but I'm not happy about it, and I'm a little angry with you.

2. okay =

a. Yes, I agree, and I'm happy about this.

b. I agree, but I'm not happy about it, and I'm a little angry with you.

3. you're kidding =

   a. This surprises me, but I believe you.

   b. I think you're making a joke and you're not telling me the truth.

4. you're kidding =

   a. I don't believe you. It can't be true.

   b. This surprises me, but I believe you.

After Listening

A. Comprehension Check. (Pair)   What do Jennifer, Brandon, and Tanya believe about animals' emotions and intelligence?

B. Vocabulary: Words for Emotion. (Pair)   Fill in this chart with nouns and adjectives. Use a dictionary if necessary. When you finish, write an adjective under each picture on page 99. Compare your answers with a partner's.

Nouns	Adjectives
amazement	amazed
anger	_____
_____	confused
embarrassment	_____
fear	fearful/afraid
_____	happy
pride	_____
sadness	_____
_____	satisfied
_____	skeptical

a. _____   b. _____   c. _____

d. _____   e. _____   f. _____

g. _____   h. _____

C. Interviewing.   Find a classmate who has (or had) a pet—an animal such as a dog, cat, or bird. Interview this person about the pet. Does (did) the pet show emotions? If so, which ones? How does (did) the pet show these emotions? Complete the chart.

Person's Name	Type of Pet	Emotions	How the Pet Shows Emotions
Kenji	cat	sadness	just sat by the window for days after sister cat died

D. Reporting Interview Results.   (Class)   Report to the class. What did you find out in your interview?

⠿ Part Three   The Mechanics of Listening and Speaking

Intonation

Statements and Questions (Audio)

In conversation, people often change a statement into a question simply by making their voice go up at the end. This intonation shows the speaker's belief that the information in the statement is true. The speaker, however, just wants to check or to make sure.

Example: **Statement:**   Mr. Jensen isn't in town.

   Question: Mr. Jensen isn't in town?

A statement doesn't require (need) an answer. A question *does* require an answer.

A. Practice. (Audio) Listen to each sentence. Is it a statement or a question? Check (✓) the correct answer.

	Statement	Question			Statement	Question
1.	_____	_____		**5.**	_____	_____
2.	_____	_____		**6.**	_____	_____
3.	_____	_____		**7.**	_____	_____
4.	_____	_____		**8.**	_____	_____

Language Function

Responding to a Negative Question: Agreeing (Audio)

In many languages, when people agree with a negative question, they say "yes" because they're thinking: "Yes. That's correct." They are agreeing with the speaker. However, in English, the answer is "no." People are agreeing with the situation when they say "no." Here is an example:

Q: Mr. Jensen isn't in town?
A: No.

After this "no," it's possible to add a short answer. Here are two examples:

Q: Mr. Jensen isn't in town?
A: No, he isn't.

Q: You don't have a pet?
A: No, I don't.

It's also helpful to add more information. Here are some examples:

Q: Mr. Jensen isn't in town?
A: No. He's away on vacation.

Q: You don't have a pet?
A: No. I'm allergic to dogs and cats.

Q: You don't like cats?
A: No. They're so independent.

B. Practice. **Pair** One of you is Student A, and the other is Student B. Take turns asking the questions in your box. Follow the directions in your box. You will *agree* in your answers, and use "no."

Examples: **Question:**   You don't know them?

  Answer: No, I don't.

  Question: You've never been to a zoo?

  Answer: No. I hate to see animals in cages.

Student A

• Ask your partner these questions. Make sure your voice goes up at the end.

  1. Today isn't Sunday?

  2. You're not from Xenrovia?

  3. He can't speak Swahili?

  4. They aren't here yet?

  5. I shouldn't try it?

  6. She won't be able to do it?

• Answer your partner's questions. *Agree* and use a short answer. You can add more information.

Student B

• Answer your partner's question. *Agree* and use a short answer. You can add more information.

• Ask your partner these questions:

  1. She doesn't like dogs?

  2. You didn't find it?

  3. You haven't taken Biology 121?

  4. You haven't seen my book?

  5. You don't know him?

  6. He doesn't have a cat?

Language Function

Responding to a Negative Question: Disagreeing (Audio)

Sometimes the person who asks a negative question is incorrect, so the other person disagrees. In this case, the answer is "yes." It's important to use emphasis in the voice. Notice the intonation in these questions and the emphasis in the answers. Here are some examples:

Q: You mean you don't like cats?
A: *Yes,* I *do.*

Q: Tom isn't in your biology class?
A: *Yes,* he *is.*

Q: You didn't see that movie?
A: *Yes,* we *did.*

Q: She can't speak English?
A: *Yes,* she *can.*

Q: They won't be able to do it?
A: *Yes,* they *will.*

The emphasis in the voice is important. Without it, the meaning is unclear.

C. Practice. **Pair** With a partner, go back to page 102. Do Exercise B again. This time in your answers, you *dis*agree (and use a short answer).

D. Practice. **Group** Make up negative questions about the conversation "That Darn Cat." Then work with two other classmates. Ask them your questions. They will answer with the correct information.

Examples: A: Tanya isn't allergic to cats?
B: No, she isn't.

A: Brandon isn't allergic to cats?
B: *Yes,* he *is.*

Pronunciation

Reduced Forms of Words (Audio)

When people speak naturally, some words (and combinations of sounds) become *reduced,* or short. Here are some examples.

Long Form	Short Form
I *don't know.*	I *dunno.*
You'll like *him.*	You'll like *'im.*
Don't call *her* tonight.	Don't call *'er* tonight.
Is *he going to* live here?	Is *'e gonna* live here?
I*'ve got to* get *out of* here.	I *gotta* get *outta* here.

People usually *say* the reduced form but *write* the long form. (The reduced form is not correct in formal writing.)

E. Practice. (Audio)   Listen to this conversation. You'll hear the reduced form of some words. Fill in the blanks with the long forms.

A: Are you _____ take Biology 121 next term?
                    1

B: I _____. Is Dr. Hurst teaching it?
              2

A: Yeah, I think so. You'll like _____.
                                          3

B: Well, Brandon says she's really hard.

A: Oh, don't listen to _____. Besides, you know, you _____
                                4   5

take it before you take 152. And it's a required class. You can't get _____
                                                                                    6

taking it some time.

Review: Language Functions

Using Negative Questions `Video/Audio`

Listen to these examples of negative statements and responses. They'll help you to do the next section.

Put It Together

Using Negative Questions `Pair`

Step One

Write five to ten short negative sentences that you *think* are true. These can be sentences about your partner/classmate, your class or school, your city, or something in the news.

Examples: You aren't from Madagascar.

   The food in the school cafeteria isn't very good.

Step Two

Read one of your negative sentences to your partner as a *question*. (Make sure that your voice goes up at the end.) Your partner will agree (or disagree) and add a short answer. Then your partner will read a negative sentence to you. Take turns asking and answering the questions with your partner.

Examples: A: You aren't from Madagascar?

   B: No, I'm not.

   A: The food in the school cafeteria isn't very good?

   B: No. It's terrible.

⠿ **Part Four** Broadcast English: Gorilla Love

Before Listening

Koko with her human handler, Penny Patterson

Koko with her pet kitten

A. Background Reading.   Read this paragraph. Pay attention to the words in bold print.

___

Koko the Gorilla

Gorillas are an **endangered species.** Only 650 mountain gorillas remain in the wild. If we know more about them, maybe we can save them. In 1972, at Stanford University, Dr. Francine (Penny) Patterson began working with a baby gorilla named Koko. Patterson and other people wanted to learn more about gorillas.
5 They asked themselves these questions: How do gorillas think? What emotions do they feel? How much language can they learn? Gorillas, chimpanzees, and other **primates** can't speak, so Patterson began to teach Koko American Sign Language. Koko communicates with her hands. Today she can **sign** 1,000 words. In other words, she *uses* these signs. She also *understands* about 2,000 words of spoken English.
___

B. *Thinking Ahead.* **Group**   Discuss the answers to these questions.

1. In your culture, how do people find a **mate**—a future husband or wife? Check the ways.

_____ They meet this person at school.   _____ They put an ad in a newspaper.

_____ They meet this person at work.   _____ They go to a dating service.

_____ They meet this person at a party.   _____ They go to a video dating service.

_____ A friend or family member   _____ Other
          introduces them to a possible mate.

2. The people at the Gorilla Foundation want Koko to have **offspring**—babies—so they have to find a mate for her. Do zoos usually choose mates for animals, or do the animals choose their own mates? Make a guess.

3. What are reasons for Koko to have a baby?

4. What emotions are the following people expressing?

- One person turns her back on another person.
- One person throws something at a TV (video) screen.
- One person kisses the TV screen.

C. *Vocabulary Preparation: Words of Love and Romance.*   Fill in the blanks in the letter. Choose a word or expression from the box. Use a dictionary if necessary.

Words of Love and Romance
choosy
in love
responded favorably to him
video dating
warmed up to
wild about

Dear Emily,

     Guess what? I have good news. Do you remember how worried we were

about my daughter Susie? Well, she's much happier than before—maybe

because she's _____! His name's Bill, and he's very sweet. I think
                              1

you'll like him. They're planning to get married in June. Isn't that wonderful?

Here's what happened. She knows a lot of nice young men, but you know

Susie. She's so _____! She doesn't like any of them in a
                        2

romantic way.

One day she and her friend Norma went to a _____ place,
                                                              3

just for fun. They paid the fee and filled out answers to a lot of questions. A

week later, they went back. They each received a videotape with about ten young

men on it. Well, they watched the tapes. Susie wasn't interested in any of the

men, except one—Bill. She _____ from the beginning. We were
                                    4

happy (and surprised) that she seemed to like him, but we didn't really expect

much. Then she met him a few days later. They met at a nice restaurant for

dinner. Now here's the amazing part. They were both _____ each
                                                                  5

other within a few hours! Can you believe it?

I didn't like Bill much at first, but I slowly _____ him, and
                                                          6

now I'm very glad that he's going to be my son-in-law.

Well, more about this later. I hope you're free to come to a wedding in June!

Love,

Dora

Listening

A. Listening for the Main Idea. (Audio)   You're going to hear a radio interview with Penny
Patterson. Listen for the answer to this question:

• How did people at the Gorilla Foundation find a mate for Koko?

B. Listening for Reasons. (Audio)   Listen again. You'll hear part of the interview. This time listen
for the answers to these questions. Then write your answers.

1. Why do people at the Gorilla Foundation want Koko to have a baby? Penny Patterson gives three reasons: two of them are here. What is the first one?

    a. _____

    b. Gorillas are an endangered species. It's good to have more gorillas.

    c. They want to see if Koko will teach American Sign Language to her baby.

2. They think, "Maybe Koko will teach American Sign Language to her baby." Why do they think this?

    _____

    _____

C. Listening for Details. `Audio` Listen to another part of the inter-
view. Then circle the answer to each question.

Ndume

1. Why did the people at the Gorilla Foundation show Koko videos of male gorillas?

    a. Because gorillas enjoy TV, and the humans wanted to make her happy.

    b. Because the humans wanted to find a good mate for her, and female gorillas don't like all male gorillas.

    c. Because female gorillas are shy with other gorillas, and the humans wanted Koko to feel comfortable with "strangers."

2. What was her reaction (response) to the video of a male in Tacoma, Washington?

    a. She loved him.

    b. She hated him.

    c. Her reaction was somewhere between love and hate.

3. How did she react to the video of a male gorilla in an Italian zoo?

    a. She loved him.

    b. She hated him.

    c. Her reaction was somewhere between love and hate.

4. How did she react to Ndume?

    a. She loved him.

    b. She hated him.

    c. Her reaction was somewhere between love and hate.

D. Guessing Meaning from Context. **Audio**   Listen to these sentences. You will hear them in two short pieces from the radio interview. What does each sentence mean? Write your guess.

1. The chemistry isn't there. = _____

_____

2. She went for him. = _____

_____

After Listening

A. Discussion. **Pair**   Discuss your answers to these questions.

1. The interviewer tells us: "Koko is 22 now and has a man in her life, sort of. His name is Ndume." What does he mean by the word *man*?

2. In what ways is Koko similar to humans?

3. Were you surprised by anything in the broadcast?

B. Brainstorming: Seeing Two Sides. **Group**   Think about this question: Is it good for gorillas to live among humans (in zoos, animal parks, or research projects)? Or should gorillas stay in the wild (in their original homes in Africa)? In small groups, discuss reasons for *both* sides of this question. Write notes here.

It's good for gorillas to live among humans.	Gorillas should stay in the wild.

C. Discussion. **Group**   Look back at Exercise B in Before Listening on page 107. Which ways of finding a mate do you think are the best? Which ways do you think are not as good? Which ways worked (were successful) for people that you know?

Part Five Academic English: Do Animals Have Emotions?

Before Listening

listening **Strategy**

Predicting

Before you listen to a lecture, think about the topic for a few minutes. Do you have any ideas or opinions about this topic? While you listen to the lecture, ask yourself: Are my ideas right or wrong? This will make you an active listener.

A. Predicting. **Pair**   You're going to hear a lecture called "Do Animals Have Emotions?" To prepare for the lecture, answer these questions.

1. What do scientists probably say about animals and emotions? Do they think that animals have emotions?

2. Look at these pictures and read the information. In your opinion, why do these animals do these actions?

An otter. Otters will slide down a hill into the water, climb back to the top of the hill, and slide down again and again.

An Australian galah. Galahs will slide down a wire, fly back to the top, and then slide down again.

B. Vocabulary Preparation.   There are words in the lecture that may be new to you. Some of them are underlined in the sentences below. Choose their meanings from the definitions in this box. Write the letters in the blanks.

Definitions
a. sad
b. joins; connects
c. people who teach animals
d. moves back and forth
e. felt and showed great sadness
f. scientists who study a specific subject
g. not wild
h. really; in fact
i. show that something is true
j. write something down or put it on tape

Sentences

___*g*___   **1.** <u>Domestic</u> animals have many of the same behaviors that wild animals have.

_____   **2.** When a dog <u>wags</u> its tail, it is clear to us that the dog is happy.

_____   **3.** She <u>mourned</u> for weeks after her husband died. She cried a lot, didn't eat much, and didn't want to do anything.

_____   **4.** She was simply too <u>depressed</u> to do anything. She just sat there and cried.

_____   **5.** Animal <u>researchers</u> are studying dolphins, gorillas, and chimpanzees.

_____   **6.** Animal <u>trainers</u> in the movies have wonderful ways to teach the animals to do many things.

_____   **7.** She thought that the bird's wing was broken, but the bird was <u>actually</u> fine.

_____   **8.** I think that my dog understands me, but it's just my opinion. I can't <u>prove</u> it.

_____   **9.** Scientists pay attention to animal behavior and carefully <u>record</u> it.

_____   **10.** He <u>links</u> these sounds with specific emotions.

 speaking **Strategy**

Using Nonverbal Communication

When we communicate, we don't always use words. We sometimes "speak" without words. We often express meaning through *nonverbal communication*—in other words, communication with hands, face, and body. (*Nonverbal* means "without words.")

- **Body language** = the way that people move (for communication)
- **Hand gestures** = specific body language that uses the hands for communication
- **Facial expressions** = specific body language that uses the face for communication

(Note: Turn back to page 99. Notice the facial expressions.)

C. Practice. **Pair** *Without words,* communicate at least six of these emotions or ideas to your partner. Use only body language, hand gestures, and facial expressions, but no words. Your partner will guess your emotion or idea. Then exchange roles.

- Yes.
- I don't know.
- I'm bored.
- Stop!
- Really??!!!?!!!
- I'm surprised.
- I'm very interested in what you're saying.
- Would you like to go and have something to eat?

- I don't like this stupid exercise.
- No.
- I'm confused.
- Please, sit down.
- I'm angry.
- That's crazy.
- I absolutely refuse to do that.

Listening

A. Listening for the Main Idea. **Audio** Listen to the lecture. As you listen, follow the outline on pages 114–115, but don't write yet. Just try to answer this question:

- What do scientists believe about animals and emotions?

listening Strategy

Listening for Examples **Audio**

One kind of detail is an example. Examples support the speaker's main points. Sometimes an example helps a listener to understand the main points. It makes them clear. Listen for the words *for example* and *such as*.

Example: It's easy to name an emotion. But it's much harder to study the actual characteristics. <u>For example</u>, in yourself, it's easy to identify an emotion <u>such as</u> anger. But can you say exactly what anger is, in scientific terms, even when it is in yourself?

B. Finding Examples. (Audio)   Listen to these short sections from the lecture and answer the questions.

1. What is an example of a domestic animal that appears to have emotions?

    Animal: _____

    Action: _____

    Emotion: _____

2. What are examples of two animals that appear to do some things for fun?

    Example 1: _____

    Example 2: _____

3. What is an example of a sound that "goes with" emotion?

    Example: _____

4. What are examples of animals that are close to humans?

    Example 1: _____

    Example 2: _____

C. Taking Notes. (Audio)   Listen to the lecture again. This time fill in the outline.

Do Animals Have Emotions?

I. Introduction: Animals that seem to express emotion

   A. Domestic animals

      1. _____

         a. Happy: wag tail

         b. Sad

             Example: dog mourned when friend died

      2. Cats

      3. Horses

   B. Wild animals at play

      1. Otters

      2. _____

      3. _____

      4. African Gray Parrots

      5. Zoo animals

II. Scientists

    A. Very few studies

      1. Difficult to _____

      2. Big difference between _____

        _____ and _____

        _____

    B. Many scientists _____

      _____

      Example: Descartes, 1649

    C. Other scientists _____

      _____

      Example: _____

    D. _____

III. Research studies of emotions

    A. Many studies on humans because humans can _____

    B. Problem with humans: _____

    C. Researchers can't prove:

      1. Humans aren't _____

      2. Animals don't have _____

    D. Possible solution: study animals' nonverbal body language

      1. Nonverbal language of _____

        is similar to nonverbal language of _____

      2. Jane Goodall lists _____

        which she links to _____ .

IV. Conclusion: Many researchers say:

    A. Animals _____ experience emotions

    B. We need to understand how _____ influence

      _____ .

D. Listening for Stressed Words. (Audio) Listen again to one part of the lecture. Fill in the blanks with the words that you hear. (Note: Before you listen, read the paragraph. Make predictions: What will the missing words be?)

Modern researchers who study emotions in humans, scientifically, believe that ____humans____

have emotions because they can _____ with _____ that they

_____ have emotions. Because other animals _____ speak in words,

researchers aren't _____ that they have emotions. However, there is an interesting

_____ for any researcher who studies human emotion; this problem is that any human

can _____ about having an emotion. After all, you can never be completely

_____ that another human is telling the _____.

E. (Optional) Checking Your Outline. (Audio) If necessary, rewind the tape and listen again to the lecture. Check your notes.

After Listening

A. Using Your Notes. (Pair) Use your notes to discuss these questions about the lecture.

1. What do scientists believe about animals and emotions?

2. Why do otters slide down to the water (and parrots slide down a wire) again and again?

3. Why aren't there many studies of emotions in animals?

4. What is a possible solution—a way to study emotions in animals?

academic Strategy

Understanding a Speaker's Point of View

Sometimes a speaker tells you his or her point of view (way of looking at something). The speaker doesn't say his or her opinion directly, but you can guess it.

Example: Most of us who have been around domestic dogs, cats, and horses think that these animals have emotions.

The speaker uses the pronoun *us*. The speaker includes himself in the group of people with this opinion about animals: Animals have emotions.

Sometimes you can guess a speaker's point of view. You can look for words that give you clues.

Practice.   Here is a sentence from the lecture. Read it and answer the questions.

Another very cute example of play behavior is from the Australian galahs. They slide down a wire.

1. Does the speaker think that animals can play? Explain your answer. _____

_____

2. Does the speaker enjoy watching animals? Explain your answer. _____

_____

Step Beyond

In this activity, you'll study nonverbal communication.

A. Doing Research

Step One

Choose *one* of these situations for a homework project.

- Watch gorillas or chimpanzees. (You can go to a zoo or rent a nature video.)

- Watch humans. (Choose a place where you can see a lot of nonverbal communication—maybe a shopping center or public park.)

- Watch humans from a different culture. (You can watch people at an international school, at an international festival, or in a foreign film.)

- Watch a TV program with the sound on *mute* (silent).

Step Two

Watch your situation for 30 minutes. As you watch, pay attention to body language, hand gestures, and facial expressions. In Column 1 of the chart on this page, record everything that you notice.

Step Three

Try to interpret your notes. In your opinion, what is the meaning of this nonverbal communication? Put this in Column 2.

Example:

Column 1	Column 2
One man hits another on the back. Both are smiling.	Congratulations? You did a good job?

B. Reporting Results. In small groups, talk about your project. What did you learn about the nonverbal communication in your situation? How much could you understand without words? Find students with the same situation as yours. How do your ideas compare?

Nonverbal Communication

Column 1	Column 2
• Body Language • Hand Gestures • Facial Expressions	What Does It Mean?

chapter Four

Nutrition

In this chapter, you'll listen to information about nutrition and discuss the benefits of a healthy diet.

Part One Introduction: Nutrition Facts and Fiction

A. Thinking Ahead.   You are going to read a short review of a book about nutrition. Before you read, test your nutrition knowledge. Read these statements. Are they true or false? Circle *T* for true or *F* for false.

	True	False
1. It's a good idea to eat a lot of carbohydrates (for example, rice and noodles) just before exercising.	T	F
2. Eating carrots will not improve your eyesight.	T	F
3. Chili peppers have more Vitamin C than oranges.	T	F
4. In the United States, bottled water is better for you than tap water.	T	F
5. The white part of an orange peel has more Vitamin C than the flesh (the part that you eat).	T	F

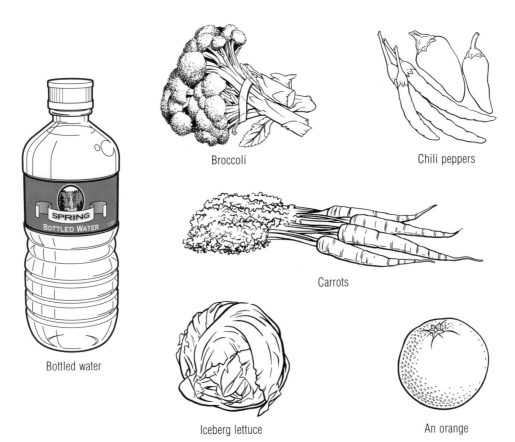

Broccoli

Chili peppers

Carrots

Bottled water

Iceberg lettuce

An orange

B. Discussion. Pair   Now check your answers. (The correct answers are on page 151.) Discuss them with a partner. Which answers did you get right? Which surprised you?

C. Reading a Book Review.   Read the following book review. As you read, think about the answer to this question:

• Why did the author write this book?

The Ultimate Guide to Nutrition
By Kristina Schreck

Are you confused about nutrition? Then you should read *The Wellness Encyclopedia of Food and Nutrition,* edited by Dr. Sheldon Margen, a professor of nutrition at the University of California at Berkeley. This five-hundred-page volume contains nutritional facts on food, advice on shopping and cooking, and information on the connection between diet and
5 disease.

   Margen wrote the encyclopedia to correct **myths** (false beliefs) about nutrition. These are just some of the myths about nutrition:

• Carbo-loading (eating large amounts of carbohydrates at one meal) improves athletic performance. (*Fact:* It doesn't.)

10 • Bottled water in the U. S. is better than **tap water** (water that comes through pipes into your house). (*Fact:* Twenty-five percent of bottled water is just recycled tap water.)

• Carrots will improve your eyesight. (*Fact:* They won't. When you eat carrots with tomatoes, however, your body can absorb beta carotene. This is a cancer-fighting
15 enzyme.)

Margen also includes a number of useful facts about food, such as these:

• The food with the highest amounts of Vitamin C is the chili pepper. It contains three times as much Vitamin C as an orange.

• The white part of an orange skin contains more Vitamin C than the flesh.

20 • The average American Thanksgiving dinner contains five thousand calories. Nearly half of the calories are from fat.

• Broccoli is one of the best vegetables because it contains so many vitamins and minerals. The worst is iceberg lettuce, but it's the second most popular vegetable in the U. S.

Source: "The Ultimate Guide to Nutrition" adapted from Kristina Schreck, "Quick Tips: The Ultimate Guide to Nutrition" from *San Francisco Focus Magazine* (March 1993). Copyright © 1993. Reprinted with the permission of the publishers.

D. Discussion. (Group) Discuss the answers to these questions.

1. Did any of the food facts or myths in the book review surprise you? Which ones?

2. What foods do you eat regularly? Do you think you have a healthy diet?

3. What ideas about good eating are common in your culture? What myths about eating are common in your culture?

4. In your opinion, is it better to get vitamins and minerals from food or from **supplements** (such as pills)? Do you take supplements? Which ones?

5. In addition to eating well, what other things can people do to stay healthy?

E. Journal Writing. Choose *one* of these topics. Write about it for five minutes. Don't worry about grammar and don't use a dictionary. Just put as many ideas as you can on paper.

- Describe your diet. Explain what is (or isn't) healthy about it.

- Is it a good idea to take supplements? Explain your answer.

- Write about your favorite **ethnic food** (food from another culture, for example, Mexican, Chinese, Italian, or American food). What are some typical dishes? In your opinion, is it a healthy cuisine?

.⠄:⠇⠇⠇ **Part Two** Everyday English: Evan's Health Plan

Before Listening

A. Brainstorming. **Group** You are going to listen to Evan, Brandon, and Victor talk about ethnic food and nutrition. Before you listen, fill in the chart. Answer these questions:

- What typical foods do students in your school eat and drink? What kinds of food can you find at your campus cafeteria?
- Next to each item, write your opinion: Is it healthy?
- What is in it? Some answers are protein, fat, carbohydrates, vitamins, minerals. If you're not sure, just guess.

Food	Healthy?	Nutrients
hamburgers	no	protein, fat
orange juice	yes	Vitamin C
cookies	no	carbohydrates
milk	yes	protein, minerals (calcium)

B. Vocabulary Preparation.   In the conversation, the students will use some words and expressions that may be new to you. First, read them in the following conversations. Then find their meanings in the list below. Write the letters in the blanks.

Conversations

1. A: That new restaurant serves unusual <u>fare</u>.

   B: Such as . . .?

   A: Such as pineapple on pizza!

2. A: Do you like the food at that Mexican restaurant?

   B: Yes, but the food is too spicy, so I ask them to <u>tone it down</u>.

3. A: Hey, why are you so healthy?

   B: Easy. I <u>do</u> megavitamins and protein powder everyday.

4. A: What <u>megavitamins</u> do you take?

   B: I take 1,000 milligrams of Vitamin C and 1,000 of E.

   A: Wow! That's a lot!

5. A: It's a good idea to have breakfast before you take the TOEFL exam.

   B: Why?

   A: It helps you <u>keep your head clear</u> so you can concentrate on the test.

6. A: Do you take <u>supplements</u>?

   B: No. Supplements are bad. You should get your vitamins and minerals from eating real food.

Words/Expressions

   _c_   **1.** fare

_____ **2.** tone it down

_____ **3.** do

_____ **4.** megavitamins

_____ **5.** keep your head clear

_____ **6.** supplements

Meanings

a. vitamin and mineral pills

b. take

c. food

d. large amounts of vitamins

e. make it milder

f. think better

Listening

Brandon   Evan   Victor

A. Listening for the Main Idea. **Video/Audio**   Listen to the conversation. As you listen, try to answer these questions:

* Does Evan worry about eating good food? Why or why not?

B. Listening for Opinions. **Video/Audio**   Now listen again. This time you are going to hear only part of the conversation. Listen to the students' comments and opinions about the foods in the chart. As you listen, take notes. Who gives an opinion about each food? What is the opinion?

Food	Whose Opinion? (Evan's, Brandon's, or Victor's?)	Comments/Opinions
chili soup		bland
tacos and stuff like that	Victor	
kimchee		
spicy food	Evan	
hamburgers		
Mexican food		

C. Listening for Details.   (Video/Audio)   Listen again. This time listen for details about Evan's health plan. Fill in each blank on page 127 with the word, letter, or number you hear. Use the items in the box.

Words	Letters	Number
ginseng	B	1,000
protein	E	
gingko		
herbs		
megavitamins		
supplements		

Evan: Well, I don't worry too much about eating healthy food because I do

       <u>megavitamins</u>.
           1

Brandon: What do you mean?

Evan: I take _____.
                                    2

Brandon: Like what?

Evan: Every day I take _____ milligrams of Vitamin C, 1,000 of
                                           3

             _____, a _____ complex—
                        4   5

Victor: That's sounds like a lot—

Evan: I take _____, too, man.
                               6

Brandon: Such as?

Evan: I take _____ and _____.
                               7   8

Victor: What are those for?

Evan: Keeps your head clear.

Brandon: I haven't seen much evidence of that.

Evan: I also have a _____ drink every day after I work out.
                                    9

After Listening

A. Information Gap.   Pair   Work with a partner. One of you works with the food label on page 128.
The other works with the label on page 220. Don't look at your partner's label. Ask and answer questions
about the vitamins and minerals in Evan's protein drink. Write the information on your label.

Student A

Ask your partner these questions about the protein drink:

• What is another name for beta carotene?

• Is the measurement for Vitamin D in international units or milligrams*?

• How much Vitamin E is there?

• What's another name for Vitamin B-6?

• What mineral has 25 milligrams?

• How much iron is there?

* Note: IU = International Units; mg = milligrams. The first seven items are vitamins; the last five are minerals.

SuperPower Protein Drink ☆☆☆

Includes all of these important vitamins and minerals!

Beta carotene (<u>Vitamin A</u>)	10,000 IU
Vitamin D	400 _____
Vitamin C	150 mg
Vitamin E	_____ IU
Vitamin B-1 (thiamin)	25 mg
Vitamin B-2 (riboflavin)	25 mg
Vitamin B-6 (_____)	25 mg
_____	25 mg
Magnesium	7.2 mg
Zinc	15 mg
Copper	20 mg
Iron	_____ mg

B. *Discussing Food and Nutrition.* **Pair**   Discuss the answers to these questions.

1. What do you usually have for lunch?

2. Where do you usually eat lunch? Why do you eat there?

3. Do you ever eat at a school cafeteria? Is the food good? Is it good for you?

4. What ethnic foods do you like? Can you get ethnic foods at your school cafeteria? If not, where can you get them?

5. Do you take supplements (vitamin and mineral pills, herbs, or protein drinks)? Why or why not?

6. If you take supplements, how do you get information about which to take and how much to take? (From reading? From a doctor?)

. : : : : : **Part Three** The Mechanics of Listening and Speaking

Language Functions

Asking for Clarification **Audio**

If you don't understand someone, there are several ways to ask for clarification. Here are some ways to ask. They are in order from the most informal to the most formal.

- What's that?
- I didn't get that.
- What did you say?
- Sorry. I didn't get that.
- I didn't understand that.
- What do you mean?
- I'm sorry, what did you say?
- Excuse me, I didn't understand that.

Less Formal

More Formal

Offering Clarification (Audio)

When people ask you for clarification, you don't always know exactly what they didn't understand. Sometimes you have to guess. To guess, you can do the following:

- Repeat part of what you said
- Repeat all of what you said

Here's an example. The person repeats only part.

A: I take *supplements.*
B: Sorry, I didn't get that.
A: *Supplements.*

Here's another example. The person repeats everything.

A: *I take supplements.*
B: I'm sorry. I didn't get that.
A: *I take supplements.* (Or: *I said, I take supplements.*)

Another way to offer clarification is to guess the word that the person didn't understand. You give an explanation or synonym for it. Here's an example:

A: I take supplements.
B: I didn't get that.

(Speaker A thinks, "Supplements is a hard word. I'll explain it.")

A: Supplements. *You know, vitamins and minerals.*

A. Practice. (Audio) Listen to the conversations. Fill in the blanks with the words and expressions that you hear.

1. A: I take a lot of vitamins.

    B: Sorry, I didn't ___get that___.

    A: I said, "I take a lot of vitamins."

2. A: I like spicy food.

    B: _____?

    A: Spicy food. You know, chili peppers, curry. . .

3. A: Did you know that chili peppers have a lot of Vitamin C?

   B: I'm sorry, what _____?

   A: Chili peppers have a lot of Vitamin C.

4. A: Many people think that bottled water is better than tap water.

   B: _____, what did you say?

   A: Many people think that bottled water is better than tap water.

5. A: I think that carbo-loading is a bad idea.

   B: _____?

   A: That's when you eat a lot of carbohydrates at one meal.

B. Practice. **Audio**   Listen to the conversations. First, Speaker A makes a statement. Speaker B asks for clarification. Speaker A then gives clarification. Which does Speaker A do?

• Repeat all of what he or she said.

• Repeat some of what he or she said.

• Give an explanation.

Put a check mark (✓) in the box for each conversation.

	Repeat All	Repeat Some	Give an Explanation
1.			
2.			
3.			
4.			
5.			

Stress

Emphasis for Clarification (Audio)

When you repeat to clarify, you need to guess: Exactly what doesn't Speaker B understand? Then stress the word. Here's an example:

A: I take supplements.

B: I didn't get that.

A: I take SÚPPLEMENTS.

Notice the stress mark on the first part of the word *supplements*. Speaker A thinks that Speaker B didn't understand this word.

C. Practice. (Audio)   Listen to these conversations. Circle the word (or words) in the sentence that the first speaker thinks that the other speaker didn't understand.

1. I said I take (vitamins.)

2. I had chili soup for lunch.

3. Chili peppers have Vitamin A.

4. Burgers aren't good for you.

5. I said, "I don't believe you."

D. Practice. (Pair)   Make conversations in this pattern:

• Student A makes statements about a topic. But Student A isn't easy to understand.

• So Student B asks for clarification.

• Student A then offers clarification: Student A stresses the word that he or she thinks that Student B didn't understand.

Take turns playing the roles of Student A and Student B. Talk about the topics below.

Example: A: I ate lunch at the cafeteria today.

B: What did you say?

A: I said I ate at the CAFETERIA today.

Topics

- My breakfast/lunch today
- My favorite food
- Supplements
- My opinion of the food at _____ (local/campus restaurant)
- My opinion of _____ food (type of food—for example, Mexican or health food)

Pronunciation

Reduced Forms in Questions with *Do* and *Did* (Audio)

When people speak quickly, some words become reduced, or short. Here are some examples.

Long Form	Short Form
Why do you want that?	Why'dya want that?
What do you mean?	Wha'dya mean?
What did you say?	Wha'ja say?
Where did you say you were going?	Where'ja say you were going?
Who did you speak to?	Who'ja speak to?
When did you leave?	When'ja leave?
How did you get here?	How'ja get here?

E. Practice. (Audio)   People say short forms but write the long forms. Listen to this conversation. You'll hear the reduced form of some words. Fill in the blanks with the long forms.

A: ____Where did you____ say you were going?
                  1

B: I said I was going to get some lunch at the cafeteria.

A: _____ want to eat at the cafeteria? The food is terrible.
              2

B: I like the chili soup there.

A: _____ say?
              3

B: I like the chili soup.

A: _____ mean? That stuff's terrible!
              4

B: That's *your* opinion. I happen to like it.

Review: Language Functions

Asking for and Offering Clarification   (Video/Audio)

Listen to these examples of how to ask for and offer clarification. The examples will help you to do the next section.

Put It Together

Asking for and Offering Clarification   (Pair)

- Student A chooses a topic from the following list and talks about it to Student B.
- Student B asks for clarification, using the expressions on page 129.
- Student A offers clarification (see page 130 for ways) and stresses important words.

Take turns playing the roles of Student A and Student B.

Example: A: My favorite restaurant is Tandoori House.

B: I'm sorry, I didn't get that.

A: I said Tandoori House is my favorite restaurant.

Topics

- My favorite dish
- The best cook to know is _____ because _____
- My favorite restaurant
- Food for a holiday or celebration in my culture
- My favorite junk food

· . : : : : : **Part Four** Broadcast English: The Mediterranean Diet

Before Listening

A. Brainstorming. Group You are going to hear a radio program about the diet of the Mediterranean region. Before you listen, write down as many Mediterranean countries, foods, and drinks as you can think of in the chart. You will find some examples in the chart.

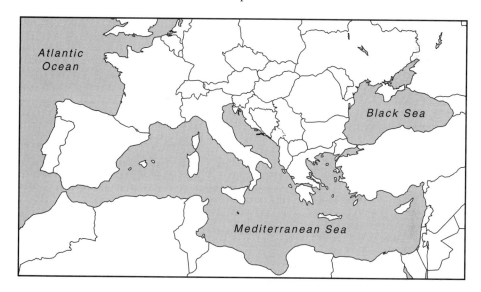

The Mediterranean Region

Mediterranean Countries	Mediterranean Foods and Drinks
Greece	an eggplant
Morocco	
Italy	
_____	olive oil
_____	
_____	
_____	
_____	

(Continued)

The Mediterranean Region *(Concluded)*

Mediterranean Countries	Mediterranean Foods and Drinks
_____	garlic
_____	
_____	
_____	
_____	an artichoke
_____	
_____	
_____	
_____	_____
_____	_____
_____	_____
_____	_____
_____	_____
_____	_____
_____	_____

B. Predicting. **Pair**   Before you listen, make a prediction about what you are going to hear. Discuss the answer to this question with your partner. Write your answer.

1. In your opinion, is the diet of the Mediterranean region healthy or unhealthy? Explain your answer.

_____

2. Now test your knowledge of the Mediterranean diet. Read these statements. Are they true or false? Circle *T* for true or *F* for false. Do you and your partner agree on all the answers?

	True	False
a. The Mediterranean diet includes a lot of fruit and vegetables.	T	F
b. It includes a lot of grains, such as pasta and bread.	T	F
c. It includes a lot of meat.	T	F
d. It includes a lot of butter and milk.	T	F
e. People on a Mediterranean diet seem to live longer.	T	F

C. Guessing Meaning from Context.   You are going to hear a radio program about nutrition. Before you listen, guess the meanings of some words from the program. The words are underlined in the sentences. Look for clues to their meanings in the words around them.

Write your guess in the blank after each sentence. Then check your guess with your teacher or the dictionary.

1. The Mediterranean diet <u>intrigues</u> nutrition researchers. They ask, "Why does the food of the Mediterranean make people healthier than northern Europeans and Americans?"

   Guess: _____

2. Researchers have discovered that Greeks have a long <u>life expectancy</u>. One study showed that they live on average 10 years longer than people in the United States do.

   Guess: _____

3. Uncooked artichokes are tough. You have to cook them a long time to make them <u>tender</u> enough to eat.

   Guess: _____

4. That dish you're preparing is so <u>pungent</u> that I can smell it from the next room!

   Guess: _____

5. Vitamin E is an <u>antioxidant</u>; it protects the body from poisons in the environment.

   Guess: _____

6. Some Mediterranean countries grow grapes <u>in abundance</u>. They are major producers of wine.

   Guess: _____

7. Fruits and vegetables shouldn't be <u>altered</u> too much; if you add sugar or salt or overcook them, they aren't as good for you.

   Guess: _____

8. Most nutrition experts agree: It's good to eat lots of fruits and vegetables. Therefore, they've <u>endorsed</u> the recommendation to eat five servings a day.

   Guess: _____

Listening

A. Listening for the Main Idea. (Audio) Listen to the radio program. As you listen, try to answer this question:

- Why is the Mediterranean diet healthy?

listening Strategy

Listening for Reasons (Audio)

When you are listening to an argument, remember that the reasons that support it are important information. Listen for facts, examples, **statistics** (numbers), or **anecdotes** (stories). These will convince you that the argument is true.

B. Listening for Reasons. (Audio) Now listen again. Why is the Mediterranean diet healthy? Find at least two reasons and write them here.

Reasons

It is low in fat.
_____   _____

_____   _____

C. Listening for Details. (Audio) Listen to a part of the program. Listen for the names of fruits and vegetables that you can find at a Mediterranean market. List them.

tomatoes
_____   _____

_____   _____

listening Strategy

Listening for Numerical Information (Audio)

As you learned, speakers often give important supporting information in statistics or numbers. Listen carefully for number expressions with the word *percent* and for fractions such as *one fifth*.

D. Finding Numerical Information. (Audio) Listen to another part of the program. This time, listen for numerical information: statistics, numbers, and quantities. Write the numerical words and expressions in the correct places in the blanks. Use the items in the box.

Numerical Words and Expressions

Numerical Words and Expressions

fifth   third

fifty percent   two or less

five or more

All the way from the mouth on down through the stomach, in the colo-rectum, and also lung cancer

and many other internal organ cancers, uh, risk is reduced by ___*fifty percent*___ or so, for people who
1

eat _____ servings a day of fruits and vegetables, compared to many people who are out
2

there who eat _____ a day. And I think that's a very important difference.
3

With cancer now responsible for a _____ of all deaths in America, the fight against it
4

is shifting to prevention. Scientists estimate that what we eat accounts for at least a _____
5

of all cancers.

E. Listening for Comparisons. (Audio) How does the American diet compare to the Mediterranean diet? Listen to this part of the program and complete the chart.

	Americans	**People in the Mediterranean Region**
Servings of Fruit and Vegetables		

After Listening

A. Discussion. `Group`   Discuss the answers to these questions.

1. According to the radio program, why is the Mediterranean diet healthy? Summarize the information in your own words. Then answer this question: Do you agree that it is healthy? Why or why not?

2. How does your diet compare to the Mediterranean diet?

3. What other ethnic or regional diets (Chinese, Mexican, Japanese, Middle Eastern) are healthy, in your opinion?

4. What ethnic or regional diets are unhealthy, in your opinion?

5. In your opinion, what other diets are healthy or unhealthy (for example, vegetarian, low-fat, or high-protein)?

B. Discussing Your Predictions. `Pair`   Work with the same partner as you did for *Before Listening*, Exercise B, Part 2, on page 136. Look at your answers for that exercise. Do you want to change any answers about the Mediterranean diet?

. : : : : : **Part Five** Academic English: Basic Principles of Nutrition

Before Listening

A. Brainstorming. `Group`   You are going to listen to a lecture about nutrition. It is presented by a nutritionist. Brainstorm for as much information as you can about nutrition. Discuss the answers to these questions:

1. What are the nutrients in food?

2. What is the connection between food and disease?

3. What are some rules or guidelines about diets? In other words, what foods should we eat? How much of them should we eat?

academic Strategy

Asking Questions Before You Listen

In Chapter Two, you saw that it is a good idea to ask questions *while* you listen to a lecture. It is also a good idea to ask questions *before* you listen. This helps you to think ahead so you can focus on the lecture.

B. Thinking Ahead.   Look at the outline for the lecture on pages 143–145 and think about your brainstorming discussion. What *don't* you know about nutrition? Write at least three questions about the subject.

_____

_____

_____

C. Guessing Meaning from Context.   In the lecture on nutrition, you are going to hear some words that may be new to you. Before you listen, guess the meanings of some words from the lecture. The words are underlined in the sentences. Look for clues to their meanings in the words around them.

Write your guess in the blank after each sentence. Then check your guess with your teacher or the dictionary.

1. Diet has a <u>profound</u> effect on health. In fact, it is so important that everyone should understand the basics of nutrition.

Guess: _____

2. Vitamin C is <u>essential</u> to good health. Without it, you can become ill.

Guess: _____

3. Protein <u>promotes</u> tissue repair: It helps tissue (such as the heart and the lungs) to fix itself.

Guess: _____

4. Too much fat in the diet is <u>associated with</u> heart disease. In fact, many studies prove the connection.

Guess: _____

5. You can eat fats and sweets <u>in moderation</u>, but too many of them are bad for your health.

Guess: _____

6. You can make your diet healthier by <u>decreasing</u> the amount of salt in your food. A diet with less salt is better for your heart.

Guess: _____

Listening

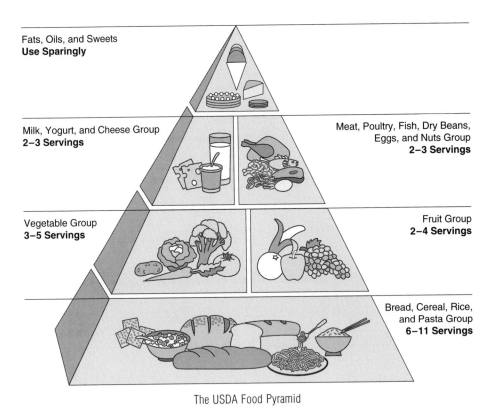

The USDA Food Pyramid

A. Listening for the Main Idea. **Audio**   Listen to the lecture. It is titled "Basic Principles of Nutrition." As you listen, try to answer this question:

- What are the nutrients in food?

B. Taking Notes. **Audio**   Listen to the lecture again. This time fill in the outline.

Basic Principles of Nutrition

I. Principles of Good Nutrition

   A. Introduction to nutrients

      1. Definition: substances from food, provide body with energy, help growth and repair of body tissues

      2. Classes of nutrients

         a. _____

         b. Fats

         c. _____

         d. _____

         e. _____

         f. _____

   B. The connection between nutrition and disease

      1. Nutrition plays a role in _____

         _____

      2. Diseases include high blood pressure, heart disease, diabetes, and overweight

      3. The government has developed _____

         _____

         in order to _____

   C. The dietary guidelines for Americans

      1. _____

      2. _____

      3. _____

      4. _____

      5. _____

      6. Use salt and sodium only in moderation

      7. _____

II. Planning a Healthy Diet

  A. Five food groups

    1. _____

    2. _____

    3. Fruits

    4. _____

    5. _____

  B. Diet planning principles

    1. Balance: eat right amount of foods from each food group

    2. Variety: _____

       _____

    3. Moderation: _____

       _____

  C. Smart food shopping

    1. Read food labels—look for _____

       _____

    2. _____

       _____

    3. Important vegetables _____

       _____

    4. Legumes: _____

    5. Select lean meats, fish and poultry, and low-fat milk

III. Nutritional Aspects of Ethnic Diets

  A. The meaning of food

    1. People eat for pleasure; to be part of family and social situations

    2. Culture influences eating habits

      a. Eating traditional cultural foods makes people feel

        _____

        _____

      b. Ethnic diets are _____

        _____

      c. The term "foodways" means food habits and customs in a
        particular culture

    B. Mediterranean

       1. The diet includes _____

       _____

       2. Most of the fat comes from _____

       _____

       3. People consider the diet to be _____

       because _____

    C. Chinese

       1. The diet includes _____

       _____

       2. It's low in _____

       but high in _____

       3. It's a good diet when _____

       _____

    D. African American

       1. The diet includes _____

       _____

       2. It's high in _____,

       which increases _____

       3. You can make it healthy by _____

       _____

    E. Mexican

       1. The diet includes _____

       _____

       2. The diet is high in _____

       _____

       3. You can make it better by _____

       _____

Source: Adapted from a nutrition lecture written by Dr. Deborah E. Blocker, D.Sc., M.P.H., R.D., CDN, City University of New York. Copyright

listening Strategy

Listening for Categories and Definitions (Audio)

Sometimes you can predict when a lecturer is about to explain some very important information. Key words and expressions let you know that important information (such as categories and definitions) is coming. When this happens, you need to take good notes.

Expressions that introduce categories include the following:

• There are [number] types/classes/kinds of . . .

• X is/can be divided into [number] groups/classes/categories

Example: *There are two kinds of* dietary fat: animal fat, such as butter, and vegetable fat, such as olive oil.

Expressions that introduce a definition or explanation include these:

• X means Y

• X is Y

Example: Foodways <u>means</u> the habits, customs, and beliefs people in a certain culture have about food.

C. Listening for Categories and Definitions. (Audio)   Listen to the lecture again. Listen for the expressions that introduce categories and definitions or explanations. Write your answer to the questions.

1. How many classes of nutrients are there? _____

2. There are five food groups. What do foods in each group have in common?

_____

_____

3. What does *balance* mean in diet planning?

_____

_____

4. What are tortillas?

_____

After Listening

A. Using Your Notes. **Pair**   Use your notes to discuss these questions about the lecture.

1. What are nutrients? Give examples of each type.

2. What is the connection between nutrition and disease?

3. What dietary guidelines do government and other agencies recommend for Americans?

4. What should you consider when you plan your diet? (Think about food groups, principles, and shopping.)

5. What does "foodways" mean?

6. Describe the diet of each of the following ethnic groups: Mediterranean, Chinese, African American, and Mexican.

B. Reviewing Ideas. **Pair**   Look back to your questions in Exercise B in *Before Listening* on page 141. Read them to your partner. Can you now answer any of the questions?

C. Discussion. **Group**   Try to form groups of students from different ethnic backgrounds. Discuss the answers to these questions.

1. **The Five Food Groups:** The Five Food Groups is a program from the United States Department of Agriculture. The examples in the lecture are from the North American diet. Give an example from each food group from *your* culture or country.

2. **Dietary Guidelines for Americans:** Do you agree with these? Do the guidelines seem international to you, or are they best for Americans only? Are these guidelines good for your native country or ethnic group? Why or why not?

3. **Nutritional Aspects of Ethnic Diets:** Dr. Blocker, the lecturer, is critical of some aspects of ethnic diets. Do you agree with her, or is she mistaken?

 academic Strategy

Comparing Information

Sometimes in college, you get information on a topic from more than one place. For example, you may get information from a professor and from a textbook.

Sometimes the information may not seem to agree. You may want to ask your professor about this. Or you may look for more information in other places. You should look for current information. You should look for information from experts in the field. For example, a book by a nutritionist should give correct information on nutrition.

Practice. **Pair** Discuss the answers to these questions.

1. Both the broadcast and lecture gave information about the Mediterranean diet. Look at your notes. Look back at Part Four. Did the lecture give you any new information about the diet?

2. The broadcast said that the Mediterranean diet was low in fat. The lecturer, however, said the Mediterranean diet was actually high in fat—but the fat was from olive oil. Read the following passage from a book by a nutritionist. What are your ideas about fat and the Mediterranean diet now?

   The Mediterranean diet has fat—olive oil. Research shows that olive oil is rich in a type of fat that does not raise "bad" cholesterol. "Bad" cholesterol is the kind that leads to heart disease. In addition, olive oil has a lot of Vitamin E. This vitamin protects the heart from "bad" cholesterol.

Step Beyond

You are going collaborate (work together) with a small group to create a meal that will both

- Taste good to people from different ethnic groups
- Be healthy

A. Taking a Survey.   Conduct a survey of all of your classmates. Ask the following questions. Complete a chart like the one on page 149.

Questions

1. What is your native country or culture?

2. What are your favorite foods in each of these food groups?

   a. Bread, cereals, and other grain products

   b. Vegetables

   c. Fruits

   d. Meat, poultry, fish, and alternatives (alternatives are protein from plants such as soybeans)

   e. Milk, cheese, and yogurt

	Bread, Cereals, and Other Grain Products	Vegetables	Fruits	Meat, Fish Poultry	Milk, Cheese and Yogurt
Name _____ Country _____					
Name _____ Country _____					
Name _____ Country _____					
Name _____ Country _____					
Name _____ Country _____					
Name _____ Country _____					
Name _____ Country _____					
Name _____ Country _____					

speaking Strategy

Taking Turns

When you collaborate in a group, it's important to take turns talking. If you like to talk, make sure to give the quieter group members a chance to speak. You can help them by asking them for their opinions. If you don't like to talk, force yourself to make at least one comment. If you are shy, sometimes it helps to write down your ideas first, and then say them.

B. Planning a Menu Group

Step One

Now get into small groups. Share the findings from your survey. Make sure that everyone in the group has a chance to talk. Use the survey results to create a meal with dishes from each of the five groups. Choose dishes that your classmates like. Write a menu using the form on page 151.

Step Two

List the nutrients of each dish on your menu. In other words, indicate the amount of protein, fat, carbohydrates, and vitamins and minerals in each item.

To find out the nutrients for the items on your menu, try the following:

- Use the nutrition information that appears on most food packaging in the United States (see the example at the right).

- Get the information from a book on nutrition at the library.

- Find nutrition information on the Internet. Try the United States Department of Agriculture's website <http://www.usda.gov>.

After you do the research, review your menu. Do you want to change some items for a healthier meal?

Nutrition Facts		
Serving Size 1/2 cup (56g)		
Servings per Container 8		
Amount per Serving		
Calories 200 Calories from Fat 10		
		% Daily Value*
Total Fat 1g		**2%**
Saturated Fat 0g		**0%**
Cholesterol 0mg		**0%**
Sodium 0mg		**0%**
Total Carbohydrate 41g		**14%**
Dietary Fiber 2g		**8%**
Sugars 1g		
Protein 7g		
Vitamin A 0%	▪	Vitamin C 0%
Calcium 0%	▪	Iron 10%
Thiamin 35%	▪	Riboflavin 15%
Niacin 20%	▪	Folic acid 30%

*Percent Daily Values are based on a 2,000 calorie diet. Your daily values may be higher or lower depending on your calorie needs.

		Calories:	2,000	2,500
Total Fat	Less than		65g	80g
Sat Fat	Less than		20g	25g
Cholesterol	Less than		300mg	300mg
Sodium	Less than		2,400mg	2,400mg
Total Carbohydrate			300g	375g
Dietary Fiber			25g	30g

Calories per gram
Fat 9   Carbohydrate 4   Protein 4

Nutrition label from a package of pasta

Menu

Dish	Nutrients
Item 1:	
Item 2:	
Item 3:	
Item 4:	
Item 5:	

C. Discussing Survey Results. Class

Make copies of your menu. Pass it around the class. Have the class vote on the best meal. Discuss why it is the best.

Answers for page 120

Answers: 1. F   2. T   3. T   4. F   5. T

unit
3

U.S. History

chapter Five

The Days of Slavery

In this chapter, you'll listen to information and discuss the history of slavery in the United States. You'll also learn about people who were against slavery and who were in the antislavery movement.

Part One Introduction: Fighting against Slavery

A. Studying Historical Information. (Pair)   Look at the pictures. Then read the passage on page 158. It describes the life of a slave, Solomon Northup, an escaped slave. Slaves like Northup worked long hours in the field and picked cotton. Then discuss these questions.

1. What did you learn about the life of slaves in the United States from the pictures?

2. What did you learn from the passage?

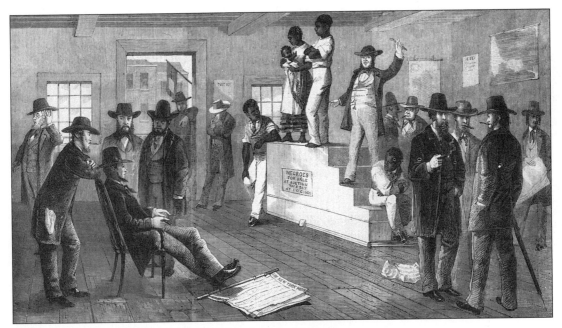

A slave auction

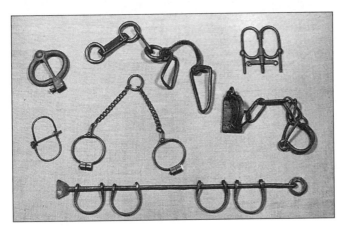

Slave shackles

A slave identification tag

A plantation

Slaves cutting
sugarcane

Weighing cotton

Solomon Northup's Story

The slaves must be in the cotton fields as soon as it is light in the morning. Except for the ten or fifteen minutes that they get at noon, they are not allowed to rest until it is too dark to see. When the moon is full, they often work till the middle of the night . . .

5   When the day's work is finished, they carry their baskets to the gin-house,[1] where the cotton is weighed. No matter how much a slave longs for[2] sleep and rest, he never approaches the gin-house without fear. If the basket does not weigh enough, the slave knows that he must suffer.

[1] gin-house: a place on a plantation where a machine separated usable parts of cotton from unusable parts

[2] longs for: deeply desires, wants

B. Thinking Ahead.   **Group**   You are going to read a short biography of Frederick Douglass, a famous escaped slave. Before you read, share any information you have about slavery with your group members. Discuss the answers to these questions.

1. What societies in history had slavery?

2. When did it exist?

3. Why did it exist?

4. Does it exist anywhere today?

C. Reading a Biography.   Read the following biography of Frederick Douglass. As you read, try to answer this question:

• What did Douglass fight for during his lifetime?

Frederick Douglass
(1817–1895)

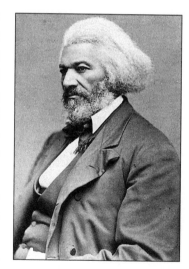

In 1838, Frederick Douglass escaped from slavery in Tuckahoe, Maryland, for freedom in New Bedford, Massachusetts. Northern states like Massachusetts did not have slavery at
5 this time, and so slaves from Southern slave states like Maryland could go to the North and be free. However, Southern slave owners sometimes found their slaves in the North, and they could legally ask for them back.

10   In 1840, at a meeting of the Massachusetts Antislavery Society, Douglass talked about the meaning of freedom. The **abolitionists**[1] hired him to give public speeches about his life as a slave. Douglass worked for the end of slavery
15 and the end of unfair treatment of African Americans everywhere.

Douglass wrote his autobiography in 1845. Because of his growing fame, he was concerned that some people might try to send him back to slavery. So he went to Europe for two years. In England and Ireland, Douglass spoke to abolitionist groups.

[1] abolitionists = people who worked to end slavery

States with
slavery and states
without slavery in
the early 1800s

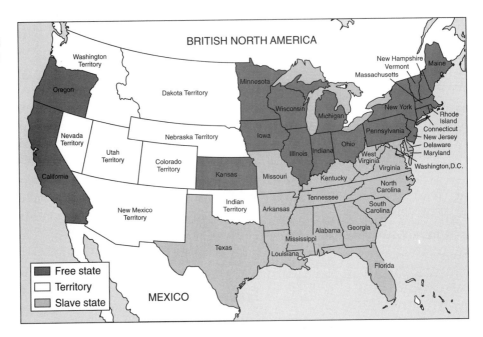

20   Douglass had enough money from his book to buy his freedom, so he returned
to the United States and settled in Rochester, New York. Douglass continued to
work for the antislavery movement. He started a newspaper, the *North Star*. And
he continued to work against **discrimination**[2] toward African Americans.

        Douglass fought against separate schools and separate seating for African
25 Americans and whites on trains. He worked hard for equal rights for African
Americans. Douglass was the leading supporter of liberty and justice for African
Americans in the 1800s.

[2] discrimination = unfair treatment

Source: "Frederick Douglass," adapted from Henry N. Drewry and Thomas H. O'Connor, *America Is.* Copyright © 1995 by Glencoe
Publishing Company. Reprinted with the permission of Glencoe/McGraw-Hill, Inc.

D. Discussion. Group   Discuss the answers to these questions.

1. Do you know about any other events in U.S. history that took place during the time of slavery
   in the United States (1619–1865)? Share your information with your group members.

2. What important events took place in other parts of the world between 1619 and 1865?

3. What societies in history have treated certain groups unfairly? Tell about them.

4. Is there a person in the history of another country who worked to end unfair treatment of a
   certain group of people? Tell about him or her.

E. Journal Writing. Choose *one* of these topics. Write about it for five minutes. Don't worry about grammar and don't use a dictionary. Just put as many ideas as you can on paper.

- Write about anything that you know about slavery in the United States.

- Describe unfair treatment of a group of people in the United States or any other country, in the present or in the past.

- Describe a famous person from any country or time who worked to end unfair treatment of a certain group of people.

. : : : : **Part Two** Everyday English: About That Assignment

Before Listening

A. Discussion. **Group** You are going to listen to Chrissy talk to a professor about the antislavery movement in U.S. history. Before you listen, get more information about slavery. Learn the answers to these questions: Who was *against* slavery in the United States? Who was *for* slavery? What were their reasons? Follow these steps:

1. Get into two groups, A and B.

2. Read the paragraph for your group only.

3. After you read, work with a partner from the other group. Ask and answer the questions in your box.

4. Then share information as a class.

Group A

- Read this paragraph. Use it to answer Group B's questions.

Paragraph A: Northern Attitudes toward Slavery

People in the North had **mixed**[1] feelings about slavery. Not all northern whites were against it. In fact, most Northerners **were prejudiced against**[2] blacks, both free blacks in the North and slaves in the South. Some Northerners simply didn't want slavery to come to new parts of the country. Others had stronger feelings: They wanted all slavery to end. These people were called abolitionists. Free blacks, such as Sojourner Truth and Frederick Douglass, had even stronger feelings. They wanted not only freedom for black people but also equal treatment.

[1] mixed: different kinds of

[2] were prejudiced against: had negative opinions without any real knowledge or experience with

• Ask someone in Group B these questions.

   1. How did Southerners feel about abolitionists?

   2. What were some of the reasons in favor of slavery?

   3. What was one of the causes of the American Civil War (the war between the states)?

Group B

• Read this paragraph. Use it to answer Group A's questions.

Paragraph B: Southern Attitudes toward Slavery

The Southern whites hated the abolitionists. Southern leaders tried to keep abolitionists and their ideas out of their states. Most Southerners favored slavery. They had many arguments in favor of it. They believed it was necessary for the economy not only of the South but for the whole country. They argued that slavery had existed in many societies in the past. They also said that the working conditions of slaves were better than the working conditions of Northern factory workers. These growing differences between the North and the South on the issue of slavery was one of the causes of the American Civil War, the war between the states in the 1860s.

Source: "Northern Attitudes toward Slavery" and "Southern Attitudes toward Slavery" adapted from Henry N. Drewry and Thomas H. O'Connor, *America Is.* Copyright © 1995 by Glencoe Publishing Company. Reprinted with the permission of Glencoe/McGraw-Hill, Inc.

• Ask someone in Group A these questions.

   1. How did Northerners feel about slavery?

   2. How did most Northerners feel about blacks?

   3. What were some different opinions among Northerners about slavery?

B. Vocabulary Preparation.   Chrissy and the professor use some words and expressions that may be new to you. First, read them in the following sentences. Then match the words and expressions with their definitions. Write the letter of the definition next to the correct word.

Sentences

1. The assignment asks you to <u>analyze</u> the causes of the American Civil War.

2. Chrissy got an "A" on her presentation because her ideas were well <u>laid-out</u>.

3. Most members of the antislavery movement were from the northern <u>regions</u> of the United States, especially New England states like Massachusetts.

4. Some women were involved in the antislavery movement; in fact, many of them played a very important <u>role</u> in freeing blacks.

5. Why <u>were</u> some women <u>motivated</u> to work against slavery? Perhaps it was because they were interested in women's rights.

Words	Definitions
_____*d*_____ **1.** analyze	*a.* geographical areas
_____ **2.** laid-out	*b.* part
_____ **3.** regions	*c.* strongly wanted to take action
_____ **4.** role	*d.* explain
_____ **5.** were motivated	*e.* presented in an organized way

Listening

A. Listening for the Main Idea. **Video/Audio**   Listen to the conversation. As you listen, try to answer this question:

• What is Chrissy's assignment?

B. Listening for Important Names. (Video/Audio)   Now listen again to part of the conversation. Listen for the names of the people in the antislavery movement. As you listen, put the names of the people in the list into the category that best describes them. There may be more than one category for some people.

People

James Russell Lowell   John Greenleaf Whittier

Lucretia Mott   Sojourner Truth

Frederick Douglass   The Grimké sisters

Free Blacks	Women	New England Poets

After Listening

A. Information Gap. (Pair)   Work with a partner. One of you works on page 165. The other works on page 221. Don't look at your partner's page.

You are going to discuss U.S. and world history during the days of slavery in the United States. You will ask each other questions and complete a time line. Take turns asking and answering questions.

Student A

Ask:

- What happened in [year]?

- What happened from [year] to [year]?

- When did [event] happen? OR: When was [event]?

Events in U.S. History, 1619 to 1865

Year(s)	Event
1619	The first Africans arrived in Virginia.
1775	_____
1775–1783	The American war for independence occurred.
_____	Several European nations ended slavery.
1831	Nat Turner led a major slave revolt.
1832	_____
1833	The American Anitslavery Society was formed.
_____	President Lincoln issued the **Emancipation Proclamation,** an announcement that all slaves were free.
1861–1865	_____
1865	Lincoln was **assassinated** (murdered).

B. Discussion. **Pair**   Discuss the answers to these questions.

1. What new information about slavery did you learn so far in this chapter?

2. What new information about U.S. history did you learn so far in this chapter?

. : : : : : **Part Three** The Mechanics of Listening
                                     and Speaking

Language Functions

Introducing Yourself to Someone Who Doesn't Remember You   Audio

Sometimes you have to introduce yourself to someone who should know you. However, this person forgets your name or doesn't recognize you. To introduce yourself, add extra information. Here are some examples:

- Hi. I'm Dawn. I'm in your History class.
- Hi. I'm Dawn Wu. We met last week.
- Hello. You may not recognize me. My name is Dawn.

Responding to an Introduction   Audio

There are several ways to respond to an introduction when the person gives extra information to help you. Here are some examples:

- Oh, yeah, sure. Hi, Dawn.
- Hi, Dawn. Nice to meet you.
- Oh, yes, hello, Dawn.
- Hi, Dawn. Nice to see you again.
- Oh, yes, Dawn. I'm sorry. I didn't recognize you at first.

A. Practice.   Audio   Listen to these conversations. Fill in the blanks with the words and expressions that you hear.

1. A: Hi, I'm John. I'm _____.

   B: Oh, yeah, sure. Hi, John.

2. A: Hello. You _____. My name is John.

   B: Oh, yes, hello, John.

3. A: Hi. I'm John Martinez. We met last week.

   B: Hi, John. _____.

4. A: Hi. I'm John.

   B: _____.

5. A: Hi, I'm John. I'm in your English class.

   B: I'm sorry. _____.

B. Practice. Pair   Take turns playing the roles of Student A and Student B.

Student A

Introduce yourself to Student B in each of the following ways.

Situation 1: You met him or her at a party last week.

Situation 2: You're in Student B's American History class.

Situation 3: Last week, you bumped into Student B and knocked all his/her books and papers
onto the floor.

Student B

Situation 1: You remember meeting Student A at the party last week.

Situation 2: You don't recognize Student A.

Situation 3: At first you don't remember Student A, but after he or she reminds you of what
happened last week, you remember.

Language Function

Identifying Yourself on the Phone Audio

When you make a call, there are several ways of identifying yourself. Here are some examples. The
last example is formal. You use it when you don't know the person you are calling very well.

- Hi. It's Maria.
- Hi. It's Maria Taylor.
- Hello. This is Maria Taylor.

C. Practice. Audio   Listen to these phone conversations. Fill in the blanks with the words and
expressions that you hear.

1. A: _____?

    B: Hi. It's Dawn Wu. Is this Jim?

    A: _____, Dawn.

2. A: Hello?

　　B: Hi, Jim. _____.

　　A: Oh, hi, Dawn.

3. A: Hello?

　　B: Hello. _____.

　　A: _____, Dawn.

Pronunciation

/ɪ/ vs. /i/ 〔Audio〕

Some learners of English have problems with the sounds /ɪ/ and /i/. They may not hear the difference between the two sounds, or they may not be able to pronounce the two sounds correctly.

Here is an example of the difference in the two sounds:

/ɪ/	/i/
Sit down.	Have a seat.

Here are some more examples:

/ɪ/	/i/
bit	beat
sick	seek
his	he's

Notice the different spellings for the /i/ sound. These are the most common spellings for this sound.

D. Practice. 〔Audio〕   Listen to the following words. Circle the word that you hear.

1.	bit	beat		**6.**	sit	seat
2.	bin	bean		**7.**	it	eat
3.	pick	peek		**8.**	live	leave
4.	his	he's		**9.**	dip	deep
5.	pick	peak		**10.**	mitt	meat

E. Practice. **Pair**   Say one of the words on the list. (Don't say the words in order.) Your partner will write the word. Check each word to see if it matches. If you didn't say it correctly, try again. Then exchange roles.

Word List			
sit	mitt	meet	meat
seat	bit	bean	beet
pick	his	he's	peek
peak	it	eat	live
leave	dip	sick	seek

F. Practice. **Class**   Now use words with these sounds in conversations. Interview your classmates. Use the following questions or use the Word List in Exercise E above to make up your own. Write your classmates' names in the right column in the chart below. Which student collects the most names?

Find someone who . . .	Names
• <u>lived</u> on a farm	
• likes to <u>read</u> history books	
• knows the dates of the <u>Civil</u> War	
• likes the color <u>green</u>	
• likes to <u>eat</u> fast food	
• doesn't like <u>meat</u>	
• has a baseball <u>mitt</u>	
• stays home when he or she is <u>sick</u>	

Review: Language Functions

Introducing Yourself and Responding to an Introduction Video/Audio

Listen to these examples of how to introduce yourself and express recognition. They'll help you to do the next section.

Put It Together

Introducing Yourself Pair

Take turns acting out these situations. One is Student A; the other is Student B. Then exchange roles. For each situation, use the expressions and intonation that you learned in this section. Also, remember to pronounce words with /ɪ/ and /i/ correctly.

Student A

Situations

1. You are an American History professor. A student comes to your office. You don't remember the student until he or she adds information.

2. You are an American History professor. A student comes to your office. You don't remember him or her at all.

3. Ask a classmate about something from yesterday's history assignment. You spoke to the person one time before a class. Your classmate doesn't remember you and doesn't remember anything about the assignment.

4. Ask a classmate about something from yesterday's history assignment. You spoke to the classmate one time before a class. Your classmate remembers after you add some information.

5. You call a friend you know well on the phone and ask about yesterday's homework.

6. You call someone you don't know well—your teacher—and ask about yesterday's homework.

Student B

Situations

1. You come into your American History professor's office. He or she doesn't remember you. You add more information about yourself. Then he or she remembers you.

2. You come into your American History professor's office. He or she doesn't remember you. You add more information about yourself. He or she still doesn't remember you.

3. A classmate you don't remember at all asks you about something from yesterday's history assignment. You don't remember anything at all.

4. A classmate asks you about something from yesterday's history assignment. At first, you don't remember anything about the classmate. Then you remember after your classmate adds some information. You remember the assignment.

5. A friend you know well calls you on the phone to ask about yesterday's homework.

6. You are a teacher. A student that you don't know well calls you to ask about yesterday's homework.

. . : : : : : **Part Four** Broadcast English: Music
of the Underground Railroad

Before Listening

 listening Strategy

Thinking Ahead to Prepare for Listening

If you know something about the topic that you are going to listen to, you might be able to prepare for listening by thinking about the topic. One way to do this is to think of vocabulary about the topic.

Example: This chapter is about slaves. I may hear some words about slavery as I listen. Some words may be *plantation, master, fields, escape, abolitionists.*

A. Vocabulary Preparation: Words about Railroads. `Pair`   You are going to hear a radio program about an antislavery movement called the Underground Railroad. Before you listen, study words about railroads. Answer these questions.

1. What runs on railroad tracks? _____

2. What does a conductor on a railroad do? _____

3. Why do railroads need tunnels? _____

B. Background Reading.   Read this passage.

Spirituals

Spirituals (or faith songs) are part of the folk tradition of African Americans. Spirituals are rich in emotion, and they express deep religious faith of the people. Many of these songs go back to the days of slavery. African Americans sang spirituals in church. They also sang them in the fields. Some people think
5 that spirituals express the slaves' desire for freedom and escape. Some people even think that slaves used the songs to signal escapes. The songs told about times for escapes and plans for escapes.

Many of the songs, however, have a real religious meaning. For example, the song "Steal Away" talks about Judgment Day. On Judgment Day, the dead
10 will come back to life, and all good people will go on to a better life in heaven. Many ideas of escape come from the stories from the Bible, the holy book of Christians and Jews. For example, the people in the Bible wanted to escape from slavery in Egypt and go back to their homeland. The situation of the slaves was actually similar to that of people in the Bible.

C. Comprehension Check. `Pair`   Discuss the answers to these questions.

1. What are spirituals?

2. What are some ideas about the reasons that people sang them?

D. Guessing Meaning from Context.   Before you listen, practice guessing the meanings of the underlined words from the program. Guess by paying attention to clues in words around them.

Write your guess in the blank after each sentence. Then check your guess with your teacher or the dictionary.

1. Jesse Jackson calls his human rights movement "The Rainbow Coalition" because there are people of many races and backgrounds in his group.

   Guess: _____

2. Faith songs are enduring; people still enjoy them many years after they were first sung.

   Guess: _____

3. Perseverance is the key to success. If you stop trying, you won't reach your goal.

   Guess: _____

4. Many faith songs are affirming; in other words, they make the singers feel positive about themselves and about life.

   Guess: _____

5. People from different socio-economic groups— the rich and the poor—joined together to fight slavery.

   Guess: _____

6. We can learn from the past how to fight some of the problems that plague society today, such as racism and violence.

   Guess: _____

7. Kim Harris brings the message of the old faith to young people, so she is like a conduit to the past.

   Guess: _____

Listening

A. Listening for the Main Idea. **Audio**   Listen to the radio interview. As you listen, try to answer this question:

- How did faith songs help the people in the Underground Railroad?

Harriet Tubman

 listening Strategy

Being Prepared for an Important Explanation **Audio**

You often hear interviews when you listen to broadcast English (radio and TV English). Sometimes the interviewer will let you know that an important explanation is coming. He or she may even ask for an explanation. Listen for expressions such as these:

- (Can you) give us a brief explanation of . . .
- (Can you) tell us exactly what was . . .
- (Can you) remind our listeners of . . .

B. Listening for an Explanation. (Audio)   Listen to the beginning of the radio program and try to answer this question:

- What was the Underground Railroad?

C. Guessing Meaning from Context. (Audio)   You can guess the meanings of some of the words in the radio program. Listen for clues in the words around them. Listen for the following words and then guess their meanings.

1. "sheroes"

    a. a kind of song

    b. a female hero

    c. a railroad conductor

2. resources

    a. historical characters

    b. bodies of water

    c. money or other things of value

3. a role model

    a. a good person to learn from or to imitate

    b. a train conductor

    c. the movement of a train

4. code songs

    a. songs about water

    b. songs with a secret message

    c. short songs

D. Listening for Examples. (Audio)   Kim and Reggie Harris explain how faith songs were actually codes that helped slaves to escape. They talk about the clues in one of the songs. Listen to part of the interview and answer this question:

- How was the song "Wade in the Water" a tool for people who wanted to get to freedom?

After Listening

A. Comprehension Check. **Group**   Discuss the answers to these questions.

1. What was the Underground Railroad?

2. How did faith songs help the people in the Underground Railroad?

3. How was the song "Wade in the Water" a tool for people who wanted to get to freedom?

B. Discussion. **Group**   Discuss the answers to these questions.

1. What did you find the most interesting about the radio program you heard?

2. Tell the group about folk songs from your culture (or another). Do they have codes? If so, explain what the codes mean and why you think the songs exist.

C. Applying Information. **Pair**   Read this piece of another song from the Underground Railroad. It's a code song, like "Wade in the Water." How did this song help slaves who were trying to escape? (Hint: A gourd is a vegetable. In the past, people made bowls from them and attached a stick to them. They used the gourd to get water to drink.)

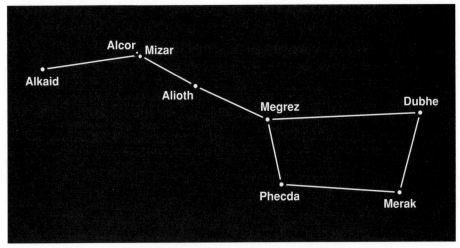

The constellation Ursa Major, also called The Big Dipper

> ". . .the river ends between two hills
> Follow the drinking gourd
> There's another river on the other side
> Follow the drinking gourd. . ."

..::::: **Part Five** Academic English: The Underground Railroad

Before Listening

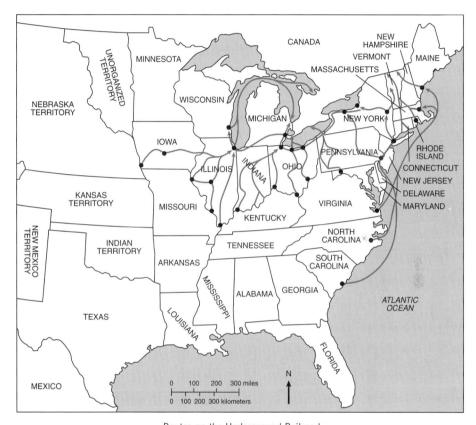

Routes on the Underground Railroad

A. Predicting. **Group** You heard a little about the Underground Railroad in Part Four. Now you are going to listen to a lecture about it. Before you listen, make predictions about the Underground Railroad experience. Imagine you are an escaping slave. Answer these questions with your group members.

1. What is the best time of day to escape?

2. Where will you get supplies (for example, food)?

3. Who will help you escape?

4. How will you feel?

B. Guessing Meaning from Context.   In the lecture, you are going to hear some words that may be new to you. Before you listen, guess the meanings of the underlined words from the lecture. Write your guess in the blank after each sentence. Then check your guess with your teacher or the dictionary.

1. Some Northerners wanted to <u>aid</u> escaping slaves. They helped them by giving them places to rest and hide along the Underground Railroad.

    Guess: _____

2. The Underground Railroad needed <u>funds</u>, so abolitionists gave speeches in order to collect money for the movement.

    Guess: _____

3. The book *Uncle Tom's Cabin* helped the movement because it <u>depicted</u> the horrors of slavery. It showed readers how terrible the lives of slaves were.

    Guess: _____

4. Abolitionists <u>denounced</u> slavery at public meetings. This helped people to realize how bad slavery was.

    Guess: _____

5. Abolitionists criticized <u>bondage</u> because they believed that slavery was bad.

    Guess: _____

6. Songs were one way to help <u>to steer</u> escaping slaves in the right direction. These songs had secret messages that told slaves how to find the way north.

    Guess: _____

7. Some people didn't believe that African Americans would help themselves to be free. However, their involvement in the Underground Railroad <u>refuted</u> this because it proved that they were willing to do dangerous things for freedom.

    Guess: _____

8. Escaped slaves' <u>first-hand</u> experiences, such as Henry "Box" Brown's amazing story of his escape, helped change people's minds about slavery.

    Guess: _____

C. Vocabulary Practice: Idioms and Phrasal Verbs.
You will hear some expressions in the lecture: phrasal verbs and idioms. Some of them are underlined in these sentences. Choose their meanings from the definitions in this box. Write the letters in the blanks.

> **Definitions**
>
> *a.* criticize   *b.* do anything necessary   *c.* first appeared   *d.* travel

Sentences

_____ **1.** The term "Underground Railroad" probably <u>came into existence</u> in the 1830s.

_____ **2.** Ex-slaves such as Frederick Douglass took every chance to <u>speak out against</u> slavery at public meetings.

_____ **3.** Songs with secret messages helped escaping slaves <u>make their way</u> north.

_____ **4.** Their brave actions proved that African Americans would <u>go to any lengths</u> to end slavery.

Listening

A. Listening for the Main Idea. `Audio`
Listen to the lecture about the Underground Railroad. As you listen, try to answer this question:

• Why was the Underground Railroad an important part of the antislavery movement?

B. Taking Notes. `Audio`
Listen to the lecture again. This time fill in the outline.

The Underground Railroad

I. What Was the Underground Railroad?

A. It helped slaves _____

_____

B. It was not really a railroad. Rather, it was _____

_____

C. The Underground Railroad began (when and how?) _____

_____

_____

II. What Groups Were Involved in the Underground Railroad?

   A. Individuals

      1. Ex- _____

      2. Free black _____

      3. _____

      4. _____

   B. Groups

      1. Abolitionists

      2. Quakers

   C. Why were whites involved in the Underground Railroad?

      _____

      _____

      _____

      _____

III. What Was a Trip on the Underground Railroad Like?

   A. What time of day did slaves escape? _____

      _____

   B. Where did slaves get supplies? _____

      _____

   C. What did they use as guides? _____

      _____

   D. Where were the stations? What did slaves do at them?

      _____

      _____

   E. What happened when slaves arrived in the north?

      _____

      _____

   F. What was Henry "Box" Brown's story? _____

      _____

      _____

IV. What Was the Significance of the Underground Railroad to the Antislavery Movement?

   A. It was a way to _____ the system of slavery

   B. It proved that African Americans were willing to _____

   _____

   _____

   _____

   _____

A stop on the Underground Railroad as slaves arrive on their trip to freedom

listening Strategy

Listening for Examples in Groups Audio

You listened for four groups (or categories) of people who were involved in the Underground Railroad when you took notes. It's also important to listen for the examples in these groups. In this case, the examples are names of people. Names are important in history, but it is often difficult to write them when you hear them because they may be difficult to spell. Professors sometimes write names on the board as they speak. It's your job, however, to connect the names with other information, such as the group they belong to.

C. Listening for Names and Their Groups. Audio   Listen to a part of the lecture again. It's about the groups who were involved in the Underground Railroad. The lecturer gives examples of people in each group. Pretend that the lecturer has written these names on the board to help you. As you listen, put each name in the correct category.

William Wells Brown	Francis E. W. Harper	Henry Highland Garnet
Harriet Beecher Stowe	Levi Coffin	Charles Lenox Remond
Frederick Douglass	William Lloyd Garrison	The Grimké sisters
Sojourner Truth	William Jones	Harriet Tubman

Ex-Slaves   **Free Black Abolitionists**

_____   _____

_____   _____

_____   _____

_____   _____

White Abolitionists   **Quakers**

_____   _____

_____   _____

_____

D. Guessing Meaning from Context. [Audio] You can guess the meanings of some of the words in the lecture by listening for clues in the words around them. Listen for the following words and then guess their meanings.

1. conductors

   a. people who raised money to support the movement

   b. people who helped slaves on their journey of escape

   c. people who spoke out against slavery

2. Quakers

   a. a religious group

   b. another name for the Underground Railroad

   c. people who kept slaves

3. the Fugitive Slave Law

   a. a law that said that all escaped slaves must go to Canada

   b. a law that said that all escaped slaves must receive a job and a place to live

   c. a law that said that slaves must be returned to their masters

 listening Strategy

Listening for Dates [Audio]

Dates are important in history lectures. It's important to listen for two things: What is the date? What happened on the date?

Listen for prepositions of time such as *in, on,* and *by.* They let you know that a date or other time expression might follow.

Examples: • *In* 1803 (a year, month, or other unit of time)

   • *By* 1860 (= in 1860 or before)

   • *On* March 16th, 1865

   • *the time* that the war ended (a general time)

E. Listening for Dates. **Audio**   Listen to part of the lecture. Listen for the following dates or time expressions. Take notes on what happened on or around these times.

In the 1830s: _____

By 1800: _____

After Listening

A. Using Your Notes. **Pair**   Use your notes to answer these questions about the lecture.

1. When did the Underground Railroad start?

2. Why was it probably called a "railroad"?

3. Why were whites involved in the Underground Railroad?

4. What was a trip on the Underground Railroad like?

5. What happened when slaves arrived in the north?

B. Discussion. **Group**   Discuss the answers to these questions.

1. What did you find most interesting about the lecture?

2. What information in the radio program and the lecture was similar?

 Step Beyond

Group   You are going to give a presentation with your group. Your group will present information about a movement (such as the Underground Railroad or the abolitionists) that people started because they wanted to end a bad situation for themselves or another group. It can be a movement from any country, culture, or time in history.

You should include the following information:

• The background or history of the movement

• Important people in the movement

• The results of the movement: Was it successful? Why or why not?

academic Strategy

Working Cooperatively

College students sometimes must do assignments *in groups*. The best way to do this is to divide up the assignment into separate tasks. Choose who in the group will do each task. Be honest about your interests and abilities. For example, if you like don't like to talk, do research. Then make a schedule. Be a responsible group member: Do a good job and do it on time.

Step One

In your groups, brainstorm for possible groups or movements to talk about. Choose one that most group members are interested in. Do some research on the movement. Do research in the library and on the Internet. Learn as much as you can. Decide who will do which parts of the assignment. Here's one way to divide up the tasks:

	Will Do Research	**Will Talk**
The History	Victor	Evan
The People	Jennifer	Tanya
The Results	Brandon	Chrissy

Step Two

Organize your ideas. Use an outline like the one for the lecture on pages 179–181. Give your presentation to the class.

speaking Strategy

Get Feedback

Whenever you give a presentation or speak in front of others, it's a good idea to get feedback—information on how well you did. You can get it from your teacher or from your classmates. If you have the equipment, you can videotape your presentation. Learn to give and take feedback in a positive way.

After all groups have given their presentations, take turns evaluating them. Use these questions:

1. Were all areas of information covered (history, people, results)?

2. Did the group do enough research?

3. Was the information well organized?

4. Did the speakers speak clearly?

5. Did the speakers make eye contact?

chapter Six

Native Americans in a Changing Nation: 1850–1900

In this chapter, you'll listen to information about the history of Native Americans (American Indians) and talk about these peoples. You will discuss the picture of Native Americans in movies and the difference between that picture and the reality of their lives.

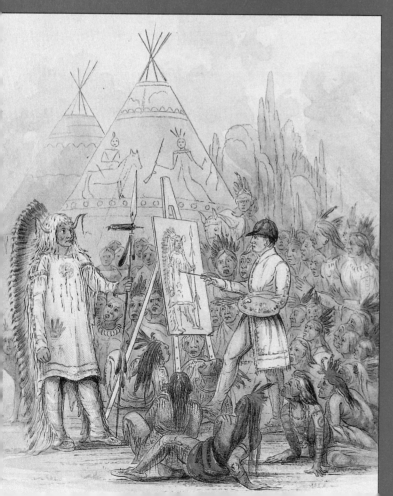

· ·: : : : Part One Introduction: Native Americans:
Myths and Reality

A. Brainstorming. **Group** Do you know anything about Native Americans (American Indians)? Where did you learn this? Discuss this and list here anything that you know. Then compare your list with lists of other groups.

_____   _____

_____   _____

_____   _____

_____   _____

_____   _____

 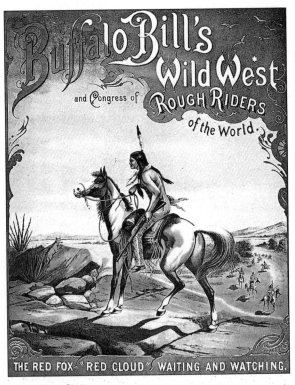

Posters for Buffalo Bill's Wild West Show

Members of
Buffalo Bill's
Wild West Show

Before the Euro-
Americans (whites)
arrived, the Sioux
tribe and other
Plains Indians
hunted **buffalo**
on the **Plains.**

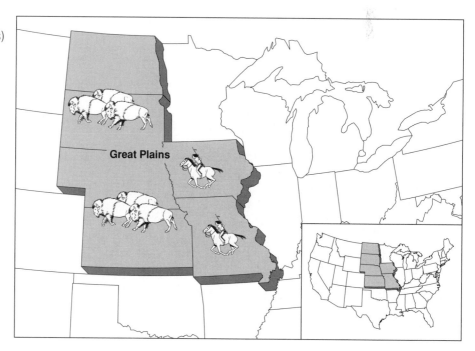

Great Plains

B. Reading.   As you read this passage, try to answer these questions:

• What was the reality of Buffalo Bill's Wild West Show? What was the myth?

Native Americans: Myths and Reality

About one century ago, Buffalo Bill's Wild West Show went on a tour of cities around the United States and Europe. It was a big success. There were cowboys, Indians, horses, and strange animals called buffalo. People loved it all. They saw Indians in "war paint" and heard Indian "warpath music." They saw the performers and their amazing skills
5   with horses, guns, and ropes. The cowboys and Indians even acted out famous battles—such as **Custer's Last Stand**—from the Indian Wars. It was all very exciting. But was it real?

A scene from Buffalo Bill's Wild West Show

The cowboys and Indians were real. The animals were real. The skills were real. However, not much else was real. The music, for example, was not really traditional Native
10 American music. And there was a lot of fiction in the action scenes. The Indians in the show were from just one region—the Plains. In reality, there were hundreds of **tribes** (groups) of Native Americans from many regions, all with different languages and customs. The cowboys in the show were all Euro-Americans (whites). In reality, many cowboys were African Americans (blacks).

15 But most of all, Buffalo Bill's show made the **"Wild West"** seem *fun.* It was not a "fun" place or time for the Native Americans. In the nineteenth century, they lost wars with the whites. They lost their land. Many lived on **reservations—**land from the government—in terrible conditions. And many lost their lives. But people in cities were always very, very interested in stories about the west, and Buffalo Bill's show was the closest that
20 some would ever come to cowboys and Indians.

C. Discussion. (Pair)   Discuss the answer to these questions.

1. In your opinion, why was Buffalo Bill's Wild West show so popular?

2. Are there any shows similar to the Wild West show today?

3. What are some skills of cowboys and Indians?

4. The "Wild West" was both a place and a time. Where was it? When was it?

D. Journal Writing.   Choose *one* of these topics. Write about it for five minutes. Don't worry about grammar and don't use a dictionary. Just put as many ideas as you can on paper.

• What things do you know about Native Americans?

• What are some questions that you have about Native Americans?

Part Two Everyday English: Hollywood and Stereotypes

Before Listening

A. Discussion. **Group** Discuss your answers to these questions.

1. Have you seen any of these **Westerns**—movies about the western United States in the nineteenth century? Have you seen other Westerns? If so, which ones? Did you like them?

2. In old Westerns, who were usually the "good guys"? Who were the "bad guys"?

3. How are recent Westerns different from old ones?

The image of the cowboy as hero from the film *The Magnificent Seven* (1960)

The image of Native Americans as "bad guys" from the film *Drums along the Mohawk* (1939)

Films like *The Searchers* (1956) show the deep misunderstandings between Native Americans and whites.

Films like *Dances with Wolves* (1990) show whites learning to understand the culture of Native Americans.

B. Vocabulary Preparation.   There are words in the conversation that may be new to you. Look at the underlined words (or expressions) below. There is a word or phrase with the same meaning in each context. Find it and write it on the line.

1. A: So what movie should we rent? Maybe a drama? Or do you <u>feel like</u> a mystery?

   B: No. I'm not in the mood for a mystery. Nothing serious. How about a comedy?

   Meaning: _____

2. Oh, that actor played *such* a bad guy in that movie! He was more than "bad." He was truly <u>evil</u>.

   Meaning: _____

3. They asked their grandfather for advice because he was very <u>wise</u>. He always knew the most intelligent thing to do.

   Meaning: _____

Listening

A. Listening for the Main Idea. (Video/Audio)   Listen one time to the conversation. As you listen, try to answer these questions:

• Do Tanya and Jennifer agree about *Dances with Wolves*? Why?

B. Listening for Stressed Words. Video/Audio   Listen again to the first part of the conversation.
Fill in the blanks with the stressed words. Use the words in the box.

bad	good (3 times)	new	terrible
better	hungry	now	think (2 times)
cry	ice cream	past	third
depressing	know	sad	this

Jennifer: That's a _____*sad*_____ movie!
                                      1

Tanya: Uh-huh.

Jennifer: This is the _____ time I've seen it, and I _____ every
                                    2   3
time.

Tanya: You want some _____?
                                          4

Jennifer: Ice cream? How can you think about ice cream _____, after *Dances*
                                                                                5
with Wolves?

Tanya: Well, I'm _____, and I feel like some mint chocolate chip.
                                6

Jennifer: You didn't _____ that movie was _____?
                                        7   8

Tanya: Not really. I mean, I know it was supposed to be sad, but I just didn't think it was

very _____.
              9

Jennifer: But _____ about all those cowboy and Indian movies from the
                          10
_____. The cowboys were always the _____ guys; the
          11   12
Indians were always the _____ guys.
                                            13

Tanya: True, but—

Jennifer: Isn't it nice to finally see the Indians as the _____ guys?
                                                                    14

   Tanya: I'm not sure. I mean, I _____ those old movies were pretty
                                            15

            _____. But _____ really isn't any _____. It
                  16   17   18

            just takes away one stereotype and puts a _____ stereotype in its
                                                               19

            place.

C. Listening for a Definition. (Video/Audio)   What's a stereotype? Tanya gives an explanation. Listen again and then write her definition. You'll hear her definition two times.

stereotype = _____

_____

D. Listening for Examples of Stereotypes. (Video/Audio)   Listen for some stereotypes from old movies and from new ones. Write them here. You'll hear the list of stereotypes two times.

Stereotypes of Native Americans

From Old Movies	From New Movies

E. Checking for Reasons. **Video/Audio**   Listen again to the conversation. Jennifer thinks there is something good about the movie. Tanya thinks there is something bad about it. What do they think? Write the answers.

1. Jennifer thinks it's good because_____

   _____

2. Tanya thinks it's bad because_____

   _____

After Listening

A. Gathering Ideas.   Prepare for a discussion about stereotypes of different groups of people. Think about these questions and make notes on your answers.

1. What are some stereotypes of other groups of people (in movies from any country)?

2. Are they positive (good) or negative (bad) stereotypes?

B. Discussing Stereotypes. **Group**   Discuss the answers to these questions. When you finish, report one of your stereotypes to the class.

1. What are some movie stereotypes of different groups of people? Are these stereotypes positive or negative?

2. In what ways are these stereotypes not realistic (or simply incorrect)?

. : : : : : **Part Three** The Mechanics of Listening
                                                      and Speaking

Language Functions

Agreeing and Disagreeing (Audio)

There are various ways to express agreement. Here is an example:

A: It's good to see Native Americans as the "good guys."

B: Yeah, I guess you have a point.

Or you can say the following:

- True.
- Yeah.
- That's a good point.

- Well, *that's* true.
- I see your point.

Often, when you *don't* agree, you still agree with one small point. Or sometimes, to be polite, you *say* that you agree before saying "but . . ." and then disagreeing. If so, you probably begin in the same way. Here is an example:

A: It's good to see Native Americans as the "good guys."

B: Yeah, I guess you have a point, but it's still a stereotype. Nobody is *all* good or *all* bad.

Intonation

Showing That You Don't Really Agree (Audio)

People often *say* that they agree, but they don't actually agree. You can often "read their mind" from their intonation. Here is an example:

A: It's good to see Native Americans as the "good guys."

B: Yeah, I guess you have a point.

Or you can say the following:

- True.
- Yeah.
- That's a good point.

- Well, that's *true*.
- I see your point.

A. Practice. (Audio)   Listen carefully to the second person's intonation in each short conversation. Does this person truly agree? If so, circle *agree.* Or do you think that this person will say "but . . ." and then disagree? If so, circle *disagree.*

1.   agree / disagree

2.   agree / disagree

3.   agree / disagree

4.   agree / disagree

5.   agree / disagree

6.   agree / disagree

7.   agree / disagree

8.   agree / disagree

B. Practice. (Audio)   Now listen again. Repeat the *second* person's response. Pay special attention to intonation.

Pronunciation

Verbs Ending in *-ed* (Audio)

There are three ways to pronounce *-ed* on the end of a word: /t/, /d/, or /ɪd/. When the verb ends in the /t/ or /d/ sound, the pronunciation of *-ed* is /ɪd/. (You need to add a syllable.)

Examples: started, traded

After a voiceless consonant sound (/p/, /k/, /ks/, /s/, /tʃ/, /ʃ/), pronounce *-ed* as /t/.

Examples: roped, picked, faxed, kissed, pitched, wished

After a voiced consonant sound (/b/, /g/, /dʒ/, /l/, /m/, /n/, /ŋ/ /r/, /v/, /z/) or a vowel sound (as in *play),* pronounce *-ed* like a very quiet /d/.

Examples: climbed, wagged, changed, pulled, showed

C. Practice. (Audio)   Listen to each past tense verb. Is the ending pronounced /t/, /d/, or /ɪd/? Use both your listening ability and the three rules from the box to help you decide. Check (✓) the pronunciation. You'll hear each verb two times.

	/t/	/d/	/ɪd/			/t/	/d/	/ɪd/
1. turned	___	___	___	**10.** saved		___	___	___
2. dropped	___	___	___	**11.** passed		___	___	___
3. laughed	___	___	___	**12.** repeated		___	___	___
4. poured	___	___	___	**13.** loved		___	___	___
5. needed	___	___	___	**14.** watched		___	___	___
6. explained	___	___	___	**15.** pointed		___	___	___
7. joked	___	___	___	**16.** looked		___	___	___
8. agreed	___	___	___	**17.** studied		___	___	___
9. killed	___	___	___	**18.** appreciated		___	___	___

D. Practice. (Audio)   Now repeat each word after the speaker.

/t/	/d/	/ɪd/
worked	worried	treated
crossed	answered	rented
washed	handled	sounded
fixed	climbed	listed

E. Practice. (Pair)   Decide on the pronunciation of these words. Practice saying them and put /t/, /d/, or /ɪd/ in the blanks.

___	**1.** hoped	___	**8.** wanted	___	**15.** packed
___	**2.** accepted	___	**9.** covered	___	**16.** pushed
___	**3.** liked	___	**10.** painted	___	**17.** nodded
___	**4.** happened	___	**11.** traded	___	**18.** thanked
___	**5.** included	___	**12.** carried	___	**19.** represented
___	**6.** played	___	**13.** traveled	___	**20.** toured
___	**7.** called	___	**14.** added		

Review: Language Functions

Giving Opinions and Responding to Opinions `Video/Audio`

Before you go on to the next activity, listen to these examples of opinions and responses to them. They'll help you to do the next section.

Put It Together

A. Giving Opinions and Responding to Opinions. `Pair` Follow these directions. As you do this activity, remember to pronounce the past endings correctly.

- Student A will give an opinion about each of the following topics. (Use the expressions of opinion below.)
- Student B will either agree or disagree. (Use the terms on page 198.) However, Student B will express the true meaning only with intonation.
- When you finish, exchange roles (Person A will become B) and repeat the exercise.

Example: A: I think *Dances with Wolves* was a great movie. I loved it.
            B: Yeah!

Giving an Opinion
Here are several ways to express an opinion.

- I think . . .
- In my opinion, . . .
- It seems to me that . . .
- If you ask me, . . .

Topics

1. The food in the school cafeteria
    (or a nearby restaurant)

2. A popular movie star (Choose one.)

3. A recent exam in your class

4. A current movie (Choose one.)

5. English spelling

6. A current story in the news
    (Choose one.)

7. Irregular verbs in English

8. A good animal to have for a pet

9. A stereotype that bothers you

10. Anything else (You choose!)

B. Listening for Intonation. **Class**   Work with your partner from Exercise A. Act out one or two conversations. Can the class guess Student B's real opinion?

. . : : : :   **Part Four** Broadcast English: An Irony
in Native American Art

Before Listening

A. Thinking Ahead: Patriotic Symbols. **Group**   Discuss your answers to these questions.

1. Here is the U.S. flag. It has a name—the **Stars and Stripes.** Notice the symbols.

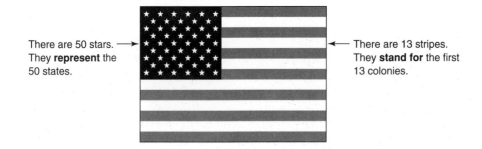

There are 50 stars. → They **represent** the 50 states.

← There are 13 stripes. They **stand for** the first 13 colonies.

Draw your country's flag and show it to your group. What are the colors? What does each part represent?

2. A flag is one symbol, or **emblem,** of a country. What are other emblems of a country?

3. Most countries have one or more national holidays. This holiday is a time for **patriotism**—love of one's country. In the United States, one of these days is the **Fourth of July** (July 4); this is the day of independence from England. What is a national holiday in *your* country? What do people do on this day?

A **parade** on the Fourth of July

4. The leaders of a new country usually write a **constitution.** This is a paper with the basic laws of the country. Does your country have a constitution? If so, what are some of the basic laws?

5. In your opinion, one century ago, how did Native Americans feel about the U.S. government? Did they feel **patriotic?** Why or why not?

B. Vocabulary Preparation.   There are some words in the radio interview that may be new to you. Some of them are underlined in these sentences. Choose their meaning from the definitions in this box. Write the letters in the blanks.

Definitions	
a. surprisingly	*e.* people in the army
b. public show	*f.* experienced fighters
c. successful	*g.* have one thing that is similar
d. public, social, or religious ritual	*h.* real; authentic

Sentences

_____ **1.** This is a <u>genuine</u> American Indian blanket from the nineteenth century. It was actually made by Native Americans over a hundred years ago.

_____ **2.** The Native Americans didn't actually use this object every day. They used it only a few times each year, on special religious holidays, for <u>ceremonial</u> purposes.

_____ **3.** He was just picking up the phone to call his sister when his doorbell rang. He opened his front door and found—<u>of all things</u>—his sister standing there!

_____ **4.** Most American <u>soldiers</u> didn't know anything about the American Indians whom they were fighting in the west.

_____ **5.** The soldiers were usually <u>effective</u> fighters because their weapons, their guns, were better than the Indians' weapons.

_____ **6.** The Indian <u>warriors</u> hated the American army, which won most battles. The Indians began to believe one thing: The soldiers had a special power.

_____ **7.** There is a wonderful <u>exhibit</u> of Native American art at the museum. Most of this art is from two tribes—the Lakota Sioux and the Teton Lakota.

_____ **8.** All of the pieces of art <u>have one thing in common</u>. All of them come from the Sioux reservation.

Listening

Art Objects by Native Americans

A blanket—a Native American woman wears the blanket over her shoulders in this 1872 photograph

A headdress—it is worn by the famous Native American leader, Sitting Bull

An example of beadwork

A Native American horse mask with U.S. flags

A. Listening for the Main Idea. **Audio**   You're going to hear a radio program about an unusual exhibit of American Indian art. Listen for the answer to this question:

• What do the objects in this exhibit have in common?

B. Listening for Details. **Audio**   Listen again to parts of the radio program. Before you listen to each part, read the questions about it. After each part, write your answers. (Listen as often as you need to.)

Part 1

1. What was real, or authentic, about Buffalo Bill's Wild West Show?

_____

_____

2. What wasn't authentic? _____

_____

3. When did Native American women begin to include the Stars and Stripes in their art?

_____

Part 2

4. One of the most "stupendous" (wonderful) objects is a mask. What was it used for? (In other words, why did people use it?) _____

_____

_____

5. Who wore the mask? _____

6. What color is the mask? _____

7. What is strange about the flags on the mask?

   a. _____

   b. _____

   c. _____

Part 3

8. What does the American flag stand for (to Americans)? _____

_____

_____

9. Are Native Americans looking at the American flag with those same ideas? _____

10. A cultural anthropologist has one possible explanation for the *crosses* on the flag (instead of *stars)*. She says that maybe the crosses refer to the four _____.

Part 4

11. What is *not* a reason for the flags in Native American art? _____

_____

_____

academic Strategy

Understanding Irony 〔Audio〕

Irony is a situation that is the opposite of what you expect.

Example: Hundreds of thousands of Native Americans lost their land, their traditional way of life, and even their lives because of the government. For this reason, it is **ironic** to find the U.S. flag in Indian art.

C. Finding Irony. **Audio**   Listen again to this short part from the radio program. Can you find the irony? Answer the questions. You'll hear the part two times.

1. What did the Native Americans know about the American soldiers?

_____

_____

2. What kind of symbols did the Plains Indians use?

_____

_____

3. In what situation could warriors use the power?

_____

_____

4. In your opinion, why did Native Americans use the U.S. flag in their art?

_____

_____

After Listening

speaking Strategy

Talking about Symbols

Here are several ways to ask about symbols.

- What <u>does</u> a flag <u>represent</u>?
- What <u>do</u> the stars <u>stand for</u>?
- What <u>does</u> an eagle <u>symbolize</u>?

Here are several ways to explain a symbol.

- A flag <u>represents</u> a country.
- The stars <u>stand for</u> states.
- An eagle <u>symbolizes</u> the United States.

Sometimes a symbol has a different meaning to different people.

Examples: <u>To Christians</u>, a cross represents their religion.

   <u>To Native Americans</u>, a cross symbolizes the four directions.

A. Discussing Symbols.   Ask your classmates their opinions of these symbols. Write their
answers on the chart.

Example: A: What does a flag symbolize to you?

B: To me, a flag symbolizes patriotism.

Object	Student 1 Name _____ Meaning	Student 2 Name _____ Meaning	Student 3 Name _____ Meaning
a star			
a crescent			
a tree			
a dove			
a road			
the color blue			
the color red			
other _____			

B. Discussion.   **Group**   Discuss the answers to these questions.

1. What kinds of folk art does your culture have?

2. In your country, do different groups of people have different art?

.::::: **Part Five** Academic English: Euro-Americans vs. Native Americans, 1850 to 1900

Before Listening

Types of **Shelter**

A typical American house in the 1800s, with a **chimney**

Typical Plains Indian **tipis** in the 1800s.
Smoke went out of the top.

A. Thinking Ahead. **Group** You're going to listen to a lecture by a history professor. The lecture is about (1) differences between Euro-Americans and Native Americans and (2) wars between the U.S. army and the Native Americans. Before you listen, discuss the answers to these questions.

1. How was a nineteenth century American house (like the one in the photo) different from a tipi? Think about the following:

   • shape (form)   • materials   • place for the cooking fire

2. Most Plains Indians were hunters. Most whites were farmers. How was the life of hunters different from the life of farmers? What did the hunters need? What did the farmers need?

3. In the nineteenth century, thousands and thousands of white **settlers**—people who go to live in a new, "empty" place—moved west. In your opinion, why did they move west? What did they want?

4. There were many wars between U.S. soldiers and Native American warriors. In your opinion, why did they fight? Why did the Native Americans lose most of the wars?

B. Guessing Meaning from Context.

There are words in the lecture that may be new to you. Some of them are underlined in these sentences. Choose their meaning from the definitions in this box. Write the letters in the blanks.

Definitions	
a. freedom	*d.* ceremony
b. moving from place to place	*e.* shared by people in a group
c. high level of society with art, science, government, religion, and writing	*f.* consider important

Sentences

_____ **1.** I value my friends, my work, and my health. But most important of all is my family.

_____ **2.** She moved west, a thousand miles from cities and towns. She left civilization far behind her.

_____ **3.** Hunters usually live a nomadic life. They can't stay in one place because they have to follow the animals.

_____ **4.** Members of the tribe lived a communal life. They worked, played, cooked, ate, and made decisions together.

_____ **5.** Many people moved to the United States for good jobs, but many others moved there for liberty. Freedom of speech and freedom of religion were an important part of the Constitution.

_____ **6.** They had a special religious ritual to protect them from evil.

C. Vocabulary Preparation: Words for War.

Match these words with their definitions. Write the letters in the blanks. If necessary, use a dictionary.

_g_ **1.** army	*a.* soldiers
_____ **2.** attack	*b.* winning (a game, fight, or war)
_____ **3.** battles	*c.* losing (a game, fight, or war)
_____ **4.** defeat	*d.* act of violence
_____ **5.** standoff	*e.* fights in a war
_____ **6.** troops	*f.* situation with no winners and no losers
_____ **7.** victory	*g.* a country's military that fights on land

Listening

A. Listening for Meaning. **Audio** Listen to these sentences from the lecture. On each line, write the meaning of the word or term.

1. be displaced by = _____

2. portable = _____

3. the Ghost Dance = _____

4. ghosts = _____

B. Understanding Pronunciation of People and Places. **Audio** Listen to the speaker pronounce these names from the lecture.

People		
Native Americans	*Euro-Americans*	*General Names for Army Officers*
Black Elk	George Crook	General
Chief Black Kettle	George Custer	Lieutenant Colonel
Crazy Horse		
Sitting Bull		
the Sioux		

Places
Sand Creek (Colorado)
the Rosebud
the Little Big Horn River (Montana)
Wounded Knee (Dakota Territory)

C. Listening for the Main Idea: Part One. **Audio** Listen to the first half of the lecture. Circle the letter of the main idea. (Note: All four sentences are *true*, but only one is the main idea.)

a. Euro-American settlers moved west and started private family farms.

b. Euro-Americans did not understand or appreciate the typical Plains Indian house, the tipi.

c. Euro-Americans tried to bring "civilization" to the west.

d. Euro-American culture and Native American culture were very different.

D. Listening for the Main Idea: Part Two. (Audio)   Now listen to the second half of the lecture. Circle the letter of the main idea. (Again, all four sentences are true.)

a. The Euro-Americans were glad to have the U.S. army in the west.

b. The Native Americans lost most battles in the Indian Wars.

c. The Indians were **traumatized** (deeply shocked) over their lost battles and began the Ghost Dance.

d. The Indian Wars ended in 1890.

listening Strategy

Taking Lecture Notes (Audio)

Sometimes a good form for lecture notes is a chart. This works well for **contrast**—in other words, for differences. For contrast, simply put a line down the center of your paper.

Example:

Euro-American Life	Native American Life
private family farms	nomadic life
independence	communal society

Another type of chart is a box with sections, or parts.

Example:

People	Year	Event
U.S. army/Indians	1890	Indian Wars ended

E. Taking Notes: Making Note of Details. (Audio) Listen again to two parts of the lecture. Fill in the charts.

1. Listen for differences between the Euro-American and Native American ideas about housing. (Hint: Listen for the words *but* and *whereas*. They tell you to expect a contrast.)

Euro-American Ideas	Native American Ideas

2. Listen for information about the Indian Wars.

Famous Battles	Year	Leaders	Who Won?
Sand Creek, Colorado			
	X		
		X	

After Listening

academic Strategy

Synthesizing Information

On exams, you often need to **synthesize** information. In other words, you need to *put together* information from several lectures or from the reading homework and class lectures.

A. *Synthesizing Information.* In the lecture, the speaker said: "U.S. troops killed men, women, and children, even though Chief Black Kettle had an American flag flying on his tipi." In Part Four, you learned about the Indian use of the American flag. Go back and look at your answers to item 11 on page 206 and item 4 on page 207. Then answer these questions.

1. What was probably *not* a reason for the American flag on the chief's tipi?

_____

_____

_____

2. In your opinion, why did Chief Black Kettle have the flag on his tipi?

_____

_____

_____

B. *Discussion.* **Group** Discuss your answers to these questions.

1. In your country, are there any groups of people similar to the American Indians? If so, who are they? What do you know about their values? Are their values different from yours?

2. Near the end of the nineteenth century, Native Americans began the ritual of the Ghost Dance. They called on the ghosts of dead relatives to help them. In your culture, do people believe in ghosts? If so, what do they believe? (Are ghosts good? Helpful? Evil? Dangerous?)

Step Beyond

In Part Five, you learned about *some* Euro-American values from the nineteenth century: private property, independence, civilization, liberty, and progress. You learned about *some* nineteenth century Native American values: a nomadic, communal life and respect for nature. Now you'll learn about some modern values.

speaking Strategy

Saying Something in a Different Way

Sometimes a person doesn't understand you. That's normal and natural. However, you need to be able to say the same thing in a different way.

Examples: They had a nomadic life. **I mean,** they moved from place to place.

Is there any minority group in your country? **In other words,** is there a small part of the population that is from a different ethnic group?

A. Finding Another Way to Say Something. **Pair**   Say (or write) each sentence in another way. Don't change the meaning. Take turns. (Student A does Number 1. Student B does Number 2, etc.)

Example: He believed that they were the ghosts of his ancestors.

I mean, he thought they were spirits of his dead relatives.

1. I thought the movie was really depressing.

2. A dove symbolizes peace.

3. The Stars and Stripes is an emblem of the United States.

4. Love of the United States was not the reason that Indians used the flag in their art.

5. They believe liberty is important.

6. What are some of the most important values in your culture?

B. Interviewing.   Find three people from the same culture (not *your* culture).* Interview them (separately, not together). Ask them about the values of their culture. (Ask: What three things are most important in your culture?) Then ask them about their own, personal values. (Ask: What three things are most important to *you?*) If the people are confused, you can give some examples. Record their answers on the chart.

* If there is a university near you with a Native American Studies Department, try to interview three American Indians. Find out their modern values.

Example: A: Could I ask you a few questions?

B: Sure.

A: What three things are most important in your culture?

B: Um, I don't know. I mean, I don't exactly understand.

A: Well, for example, in the United States, three important values are independence, work, and progress.

Culture (Country): _____

Person	Values of the Culture	Personal Values

C. Discussing Interview Results. (Group) Share your chart. Discuss the answers to these questions.

1. Did all three people agree on the cultural values?

2. Does anyone have personal values different from their culture's values?

3. Did other students in the group interview people from the same culture? Are your results similar?